Sitting at a Crossroad

Sitting at a Crossroad

A Memoir

ADRIANA FORSMAN

RESOURCE *Publications* · Eugene, Oregon

SITTING AT A CROSSROAD
A Memoir

Resource Publications
An Imprint of Wipf and Stock Publishers
199 W. 8th Ave., Suite 3
Eugene, OR 97401

www.wipfandstock.com

PAPERBACK ISBN: 979-8-3852-2920-8
HARDCOVER ISBN: 979-8-3852-2921-5
EBOOK ISBN: 979-8-3852-2922-2

VERSION NUMBER 070225

Contents

Preface

The word *testimony* is primarily used by Christian communities. However, it is not an inherently religious term. It means to give firsthand authentication of facts, an open acknowledgment, a formal statement, an attestation, a declaration. You hold in your hands my testimony.

It was not an easy testimony to write. In fact, it was a long process filled with doubt, tears, and frustration. But I was led to share it, to proclaim it, to testify. And to what am I testifying? To love, to faith, to being confident in who I am, and to a God who never let me go.

My testimony is my story. I am not pushing an agenda, whatever that means; I am not forcing my theological thoughts on anyone, nor am I declaring how others should live their lives. I am revealing my personal experiences and showing how they impacted me and brought me to where I am today.

The words on these pages are true, every bit of them. However, all names and physical descriptions have been changed unless I was given permission to not change them. This has been done to protect the identities of those involved in my story. I hold love in my heart for every person in my memoir.

I don't know who you are or what led to you picking up this book and reading these words, but I hope you will dive into this story with me. It is raw and it is vulnerable. I hope you will read it with an open heart. May you find pieces here and there that strike a chord in your heart.

Even though we have all walked different paths, there are so many experiences that simply just come with being human. Experiences of love, sorrow, joy, heartache, loss, and dysfunction—just to name a few. May we find unity in that. And remember, unity does not require complete agreement.

Some special thanks are in order for a few special people. First, to my dear friend Stitch for reading my manuscript in its earliest form and providing me helpful feedback and encouragement. Second, to my former high school teacher, now friend, Amy Schultz. Thank you for all the times you let me crash your lunch break or prep period to ask you my onslaught of grammar and English questions.

Thank you to my parents for your commitment to faithfully come alongside me on this endeavor without needing to know all the details. Thank you to the many others who are in my corner cheering me on and building me up. Finally, to my best friend Tank. Thank you for the *many* hours you poured over my manuscript and the countless hours you've talked to me about my book with love and support.

Author's Note

My chief aim in life is to bring glory to God and advance his kingdom. If you enjoy reading my memoir and are interested in having me share a message with your church, leadership team, youth group, small group, camp, or any other group I would be honored. Below is my website. Please reach out if you are interested in connecting with me.

Find my contact information at:
adrianaforsman.carrd.com

Chapter 1: Inaugural Romance

Your love made a way to let mercy come in. Your grace so free, washes over me. You have made me new, now life begins with you. It's your endless love, pouring down on us.

—North Point Worship

I sat in one of the familiar red-cushioned pews in my small-town church. The beautiful stained glass windows along the walls were uncharacteristically dull due to the setting sun. My mom had let me wear whatever I wanted since it was a casual evening service, and at eight years old I found it thrilling to be at church in my comfy clothes.

My legs were too short to reach the ground so I slowly swung them back and forth. I leaned against my mom's shoulder while we waited for the service to start. We were gathering to hear a missionary share about his ministry in Africa. When he stepped onto the stage his presence and voice demanded our full attention.

He spoke with enthusiasm and passion. I had never encountered anyone like him before. His message captivated my young mind as he spoke firsthand of laying his life down as an offering unto the Lord. He had given up everything. He left the comfort of his home country, he learned a new language, and now his full-time "job" was serving Jesus.

I knew who Jesus was. I had known for quite some time since I was being raised by Christian parents. In fact, by age four, I was already able to quote Scripture from memory. But what this man described was on a whole new level. His story and life demonstrated that following Jesus was more than just praying, reading my Bible, singing worship songs, and going to church.

This servant-hearted man described a personal decision to follow Jesus in a radical way. To give my entire life to him and allow him to guide and lead my decisions, words, and actions. Concluding his message, he gave a traditional altar call. An invitation to come forward and make a new spiritual commitment to following Jesus Christ.

I tapped my mom's arm and whispered, "Mama, I'm going up there." At the front of the church, I knelt down to pray with the missionary and devoted my life to Jesus. I took my commitment seriously, both that day and every day after. I took weekly sermon notes as I clung to the words spoken from the pulpit.

On Sunday afternoons I came home from church, looked up the lyrics to the songs we sang, and jotted them down in my notebook. I then skipped over to my grandpa's cabin next door, jumped onto his large plastic swing, and loudly sang the songs.

It was out of key, but I knew my heavenly Father was pleased with my joyful noise. Then I climbed high up in my favorite tree to find a spot to pray. Up in that tree I talked to God like I was talking to a friend. As a little girl my prayers were not structured requests or thanksgivings. They were conversations.

I told him all about my life, my thoughts, my joys, my concerns, my friends—everything. I felt his presence with me while sitting on the large oak branches. I was simply hanging out with the God of the universe. Those were some of the most precious moments of my entire life.

***** *****

In fifth grade, I had my first boyfriend. Our relationship consisted of tripping each other, pushing each other around in the hallways, and passing notes during class. In sixth grade, I advanced to a less physically aggressive relationship which involved the giving of a most precious commodity: chewing gum. On my birthday he really showed his affections by presenting me with a mega, thirty-five-piece pack of gum. Almost every day after school we talked on our family's landlines.

In ninth grade, I dated a boy who lived two miles down the road from me. Our parents allowed us to go to each other's homes and meet up in the town park. In that park I had my first kiss, and shortly after learned the difference between kissing and making out. He taught me a couple of chords on the guitar, we watched movies, and went snowboarding together.

This relationship started a trend of my parents trusting me to be alone with my boyfriends. I was a good student, I had strong morals, and I was a passionate follower of Jesus. Therefore, they believed I was making good choices. In reality, despite coming across as trustworthy, I needed accountability. I needed trusted adults in my life asking the difficult questions and having the difficult conversations. I had entered uncharted territory, and I needed help navigating my way through it.

After six months, which felt like forever to a fourteen-year-old, we broke up. It was my first taste of heartache. After a short-lived summer fling, along came a far more serious and messy relationship. This relationship proved to be transformative to my life and faith, in both positive and negative ways.

* * * * * *

All students in my high school were required to take a couple fine arts classes, meaning I had to choose between band, choir, or art. I am terribly unskilled at all three, so I picked the one I sucked at the least: art. On the first day of tenth grade, I walked into Foundations of Art and discovered none of my friends were in that class—a devastating discovery to any high school student.

Trying to hide my discomfort, I spotted an opening at a table with a couple girls I sort of knew and a really big guy I had never met. *He must be an upperclassman.* I quickly sat down and awkwardly introduced myself to the guy I didn't know. This guy—standing at six foot five, weighing two hundred forty pounds, with a deep manly voice and thick sideburns—was named Shannon.

Shannon? I've only met girls named Shannon . . . what a girly name for such a manly man.

Art class primarily consisted of free-flowing work time to complete various art projects. Therefore, we spent most of the time chatting with one another while we worked. After a few weeks of chatting, I found out he used to go to church, but he stopped after he completed their confirmation program.

"So why did you stop going?" I asked.

"Well, since I was baptized and finished confirmation, I already know I'm going to go to heaven, so I don't see the point in continuing to go to church. It's boring anyways," he answered, as if this was obvious.

I asked more questions before carefully explaining that I did not agree with this concept, and the Bible doesn't teach it either. He was shocked to hear all Christians didn't believe the same way he did. I was happy this conversation on a seemingly contentious topic stayed pleasant. He was genuinely interested in understanding more of what I believed and why. The bell rang with poor timing for the deep direction our dialogue had taken.

As we packed up our things, he remarked, "You know, I'd actually really like to finish talking about this sometime. Maybe outside of school though." He had a long-standing girlfriend, so I knew this wasn't a strange attempt to ask me on a date, and I hastily agreed. We exchanged numbers and went to Taco Bell over the weekend. On the thirty-minute drive we picked up our conversation right where we had left off, discussing the Bible, salvation, and how to go to heaven.

"I just really thought it didn't matter how much I sinned, or if I kept on doing the same sin, or anything like that, because God would just forgive me in the end anyways." His voice sounded somber. It seemed like part of him was concerned he might be wrong.

"Well, I really don't think it works like that. God is forgiving, but we cannot abuse that forgiveness. God doesn't just want you to be baptized, do confirmation, and then do whatever you want the rest of your life as if God isn't part of it. He wants a relationship with us, and part of that relationship is our commitment to fighting against sin. That is like part of what he expects us to do, you know?" I tried to sound gentle, which is not one of my strengths. "I learned a lot of this stuff from going to church and youth group. Maybe you should come to youth group with me sometime? It's a lot of fun!"

"Yeah, maybe." He muttered. "I don't know what my mom would think of me going to a youth group at a different church, though. I'll have to talk to her about it."

✺ ✺ ✺ ✺ ✺ ✺

The leaves transitioned to beautiful oranges, yellows, and reds before falling to the ground to make way for our long Minnesota winters. Shannon and I began to spend more and more time together. We discovered we went to the same gym and started working out together every other evening.

As the snow accumulated, we discovered we shared a love of snowmobiling and started snowmobiling together, too. At some point along the line,

Shannon realized he was developing feelings for me and broke up with his girlfriend. When he told me the truth of why they broke up I was flattered.

His faith had deepened tremendously since our Taco Bell chat a few months prior, and he had started consistently attending church and youth group with me. Our hangouts turned into dates, and in February he asked me to be his girlfriend. We introduced each other to our families and hung out as often as we could.

Eventually it became clear we had different ideas on one topic which created a great deal of tension in our young relationship: physical boundaries. We mistakenly had not discussed boundaries until our actions forced the conversation to the surface. Hindsight has since revealed how important it is to discuss boundaries *before* entering a new relationship.

I was new to the world of physical intimacy, but Shannon was not. Instinctively, I turned to my trusty Bible for direction, but the lines of what was acceptable felt blurry. The Bible is not specific on the topic of physical or sexual intimacy. Instead, God speaks broadly of sexual immorality and sexual purity throughout his word.

I had a distinct misunderstanding of what the Bible meant regarding these terms. I learned that, in the eyes of the Lord, being sexually pure is not limited to waiting to have sex until you are married. Therefore, navigating sexual purity requires consideration of all acts that are sexual.

Bearing this in mind, I believe there are several acts which constitute having "sex before marriage." For some reason Christians have glommed on to that phrase and it has led many to believe as long as they "don't have sex before marriage" then all else is permissible. This is exactly what Shannon believed.

Sadly, this is a set up for failure because sexual purity was never meant to be one specific activity to avoid, but a broader concept of honoring God with our bodies and our decisions. The questions should not be, "Where is the line? How far is too far?" The question should be, "Am I honoring God with my actions?" The focus should not solely be on what *not* to do, but also on what *to* do.

The specifics of physical and sexual boundaries will look different from person to person, and couple to couple. We all have different backgrounds, strengths, weaknesses, and struggles. Therefore, I find it legalistic to try to define boundaries and apply them to everyone. Even the same person may change their boundaries as their circumstances change.

Conversations on this topic, both for Christians and non-Christians, are deeply important. This should not be considered taboo, and ought to be discussed openly with trusted friends and family. Christians in particular need to discuss what it means to honor God with our bodies.[1]

It is of utmost importance for those entering romantic relationships to be on the same page with boundaries. This allows partners to respect and honor one another. Shannon and I were not even remotely on the same page. I wanted to pursue sexual purity and be sure we were honoring God with our actions, but this was of low importance to him.

I still, however, did not know exactly what we should abstain from and what was acceptable. I was in uncharted territory, and I did not know how to begin to draw up godly boundaries. I assumed once something physical was happening or about to happen, I would determine its acceptability, or lack of, and respond accordingly.

Unfortunately, I allowed our intimacy to progress well past what I felt was acceptable. In moments when situations escalated, I found myself silent. I just didn't know what to say or how to stop him without making him feel rejected. The whole thing felt awkward so I defaulted to saying nothing.

Externally I did not object to his advances, but internally I knew what we were doing was dishonoring to God. I loved God and glorifying him was the entire purpose of my life. I could hear his still small voice calling out to me, telling me what we were doing was wrong.

The still small voice I am referring to is not an audible voice, at least not for me, it is the voice of God communicating through my thoughts. In 1 Kings 19 a prophet named Elijah was extremely distraught. He felt as though he was the only faithful follower of God left in existence. God told him to stand on a mountain and he would pass by. There was a great and strong wind, an earthquake, and a fire but the Lord was not in those. Finally, the sound of a still small voice, or a gentle whisper, came, and the presence of the Lord was there.

Based on this Bible passage I use the term "still small voice" any time I distinctly feel God communicating with me and guiding me. Sadly, during this season of life I found myself ignoring his still small voice. A major conflict was arising within my heart. On one hand, I wanted to please God and do what was right, but on the other hand, I wanted to please Shannon.

I silently allowed him to press our boundaries further and further. Until, one night, I reached my limit. I got up from the couch and made up

1. 1 Corinthians 6:20.

6

some excuse as to why he needed to head out. As soon as he was gone, I went into my closet, collapsed on the floor, and sobbed. I did not know how to stop what was happening without ending our relationship, and I did not want to break up with him.

* * * * * *

"You two need to actually put your boundaries down in writing. And then you both should literally sign your names in agreement to following them," my young youth director counseled me as she sat comfortably on her gray couch. I looked over at her bookshelf to avoid eye contact as I considered her recommendation. It sounded a bit much to me, but I was desperate enough to try anything.

We had proven an inability to adhere to vague or fluid boundaries, so we needed clear black-and-white ones instead. Shannon came over and pulled up a chair next to me while I typed up our boundaries on the family computer. After a lengthy discussion, including convincing him we even needed boundaries in the first place, we agreed to stick to these new boundaries.

We soon discovered once boundaries have been broken it is extremely difficult to go backwards and instill stricter ones. It felt like trying to put toothpaste back inside a toothpaste tube. Shannon proved to be far more supportive when discussing boundaries than actual moments when I needed his support the most. Eventually, I was the only one attempting to maintain our boundaries.

I could not fight this battle alone, so we slowly began breaking the boundaries we had agreed upon. I was troubled, ashamed, and felt unworthy of God's love. *Why can't we just stick to our boundaries? It shouldn't be that hard . . .*

I confided in my youth director again. "Thank you for sharing this with me, I know it's not easy." She softly rubbed my back to comfort me. We were back on that same gray couch in her living room. "And while sexual immorality is a sin, I do think there is a different sin you need to focus on at this point: idolatry."

"Idolatry? But I thought that was more of an Old Testament kind of thing. Like with people making statues and bowing down to them. Stuff like that, right?"

"Actually, idolatry is when you put anything before God. It can even be good things, like family, school, work, or friends. Or in this case, a boyfriend. I think you have to ask yourself if you are putting your relationship with Shannon before your relationship with God." She paused, knowing her words were tough to hear. "If you are choosing to do what pleases Shannon over what pleases God, then that means you have made an idol of Shannon."

She allowed time for her words to sink in while I fidgeted with my hands. I hadn't considered any of this before. I was the kid who knew all the answers in Sunday school and youth group, I looked forward to being at church, I read my Bible often, and I attended nearly all the youth events. Now I had to come to terms with the fact I had allowed my boyfriend to take over the throne of my heart.

I had made my boyfriend a greater priority in my life than my relationship with the God who created me and sustains me. Wow. I felt like crying right then and there, but I choked back my tears because I didn't want to cry in front of my youth director.

* * * * * *

My body and mind were full of resolve. I could not stand for this. This was my first major confrontation with sin. My first experience of how enticing sin can be and how easy it is to ignore the truth, even truths I had stored deep within my heart. I was now faced with processing what this all meant for our relationship. Something needed to change, and fast.

I met up with Shannon and spewed my thoughts. "So, because of all that, we need to cut back on our physical intimacy, like, dramatically. And I am seriously sticking to this, and if you don't want to stick to this then I don't think this is going to work anymore."

I wasn't trying to threaten breaking up, I was just being honest about how serious this was to me. I was returning the throne of my heart to the one it belonged to: my heavenly Father.

Shannon was halfway through his senior year of high school by this point. He was making big decisions regarding colleges, career paths, and living situations, and it caused him to reflect on what he was looking for in life and whether or not I fit into that. I was deeply invested in my relationship with Jesus, and planned to live my life constantly open to his leading. If Jesus asked me to move out of the country I would move; if he asked me to stay I would stay; if he asked me to do a certain job, I would do it. This meant my future was full of a lot of unknowns.

I was already confident God was calling me to do full-time ministry. However, Shannon was not quite on the same page. He wanted to go to college, get a steady job, buy a home, and start a family. The thought of living his life totally open to God's will was stressful. After discussing these differences, we believed it was clear God did not intend us to be together anymore and we broke up.

* * * * * *

"Mom, Dad. I want your permission to drop out of school."

They sat across from me on our brown living room couch. Our old white cat was comfortably resting on one of the cushions eavesdropping on our very serious conversation. They immediately knew I was not joking and exchanged a surprised look.

"I just feel like school is totally meaningless. I already know I want to do full-time ministry and sitting in class is a waste of my time. It isn't preparing me for ministry. I will never be ministering to someone and need to know the quadratic formula or what year the industrial revolution began—none of it matters." I hit the back of my hand into my other palm for emphasis. I knew it was a long shot to believe I could convince them, but I had to try. I had a phenomenal GPA, a lot of good friends, and I even enjoyed the pace and atmosphere of my small-town high school. But I could *not* stand what I was learning.

"If you let me drop out then I will commit myself to a deep study of Scripture at home every day whenever I would normally be at school. Maybe I can even do some kind of online class or something to structure my study . . ."

My feisty Hispanic mom jumped into my proposition. "Adriana, we can't let you do that. We understand your frustration with what you are learning. Sometimes it can feel pointless. But you should think of your time in high school as an opportunity to be a light and witness." Her thick, black, curly hair perfectly framed her face. She smiled at me tenderly and looked into my dark brown eyes which matched her own. My dad was also looking tenderly at me and nodded to show his agreement.

Ugh, that's so dumb. I'm pretty sure every person in my school knows all about Jesus and the Bible anyways. What a waste of time.

As a typical teenager, I was upset I wasn't getting my way. My annoyance was evident to them in my face and body language. We went back and forth for a while as I pleaded my case in circles. Finally, my mom compromised. "Okay, I want you to take one week of truly and actively seeking out opportunities to be a light and a witness, and if after one week you still feel the same way then we can have a second conversation."

My face lit up with hope. *Ooh, maybe I can get them to reconsider!*

Seeing this my mom emphasized, "But you have to actually seek out those opportunities. Look for them in ways you have not before. Pray and ask God to reveal them to you. I am confident he will show you that being at school is not meaningless."

Her words echoed in my mind as I confidently walked into my high school. I sighed with boredom as I worked through an assignment in math class. I sloppily drew an alpha symbol, which should look like this: α. But mine didn't. I chuckled and angled my paper to show the girl next to me. "Look how bad that one is. It looks like a Jesus fish." With a blank look she informed me she had no idea what I was talking about, even after I tried to explain it.

The next day, my clunky lunch tray thumped onto the table as I sat in my spot by a couple of friends. I looked down happily at my third favorite school lunch: taco in a bag. A bag of Doritos filled with ground beef, lettuce, tomatoes, cheese, salsa, and corn. On the side were canned pineapple chunks and the ever-familiar carton of milk.

While quietly eating my lunch it was nearly impossible not to eavesdrop as one guy, a few seats down, was belittling a couple of Christian guys who were trying to defend why they believe in the Bible. "Wait, so you actually believe in a talking snake, and cripples being healed, and some dude choosing to die on a cross even though he was supposedly all powerful?" He snickered at the absurdity of such beliefs, and didn't show any interest in listening to their answers. I was shocked.

The large lunch room was always filled with a loud buzz of chatter and laughter. But a couple days later that noise was completely silenced as Kyle, a known "troublemaker," angrily slammed his lunch tray down so hard it broke in half. It sounded like a gunshot. Mr. Escalante, the dean of students, escorted him to the office while the entire lunch room watched and whispered. God's still small voice prompted me with a question: Do YOU THINK KYLE HAS A MEANINGFUL RELATIONSHIP WITH ME? HAVE YOU

EVER TALKED TO HIM? OR PRAYED FOR HIM? OR EVEN THOUGHT ABOUT
HIM AND WHAT HIS LIFE IS LIKE?

In less than a week, these three encounters left me convicted of my negative attitude and my false belief that everyone in my school knew Jesus. God could use me as a light and witness for his kingdom right here, right now. I didn't have to anxiously wait until graduating to do ministry—I had the chance to do ministry every single day. From that day on I pursued opportunities to be a light and a witness for Jesus. I even started a prayer group, Aftershock, which met weekly before school.

I did not change lives, I did not bring about revival in my school, but I did faithfully love those God put in my path. Jesus said everyone will know you are my disciples if you love one another,[2] and that was my goal. I happily accepted any verbal opportunities to share my faith with others, but more often my witnessing took place by the way I lived my life. My deepest desire was to be a strong representative of Jesus, to the point that my life was as much a reflection of his life as possible.[3]

※ ※ ※ ※ ※ ※

I stood in a sea of nearly five thousand teenagers packed into the University of Tennessee stadium. Chris Tomlin, a contemporary singer and songwriter, was leading us in worship. We had each been given strips of white fabric, which he instructed us to raise and wave in the air as we belted out the song "White Flag." Thousands of voices rang out a cappella on the last chorus, declaring our surrender to Jesus.

As I left the stadium, I deeply contemplated what fully surrendering myself to Jesus meant. *Am I actually willing to raise my white flag and surrender everything?* I was attending a large-scale youth event, and the previous five days had been filled with worship, speakers, seminars, small group discussions, and reflection time. At several points throughout the conference, I felt that still small voice undeniably confirming a call on my heart to do ministry.

Upon returning home my youth director invited me to share with the church about my experience. After that worship service a woman approached me and excitedly told me all about this Bible college in Chicago

2. John 13:35.
3. 2 Corinthians 5:20.

specifically designed for those who want to do full-time ministry. I promised to look into it, and I wasted no time.

Scrolling through their website I was happily surprised to find a degree in evangelism and discipleship. This degree felt perfect for me. I read the recommended classes for this program and drooled over the thought of some of the classes: Romans, Hermeneutics, Spiritual Life and Community, Greek, Hebrew, and Theology of Suffering. I would, by default, have a double major because there were so many required Bible courses everyone receives a Bible degree.

I looked into their purpose and vision, listened to video testimonials from students, and even read a speech from the president. I was coming out of my skin with excitement. This is where I wanted to go.

My parents, specifically my mom, warned against putting all my eggs in one basket. But after visiting the campus I was sure this was the college for me. During my guided tour I was told the acceptance rate was approximately one out of five. In a leap of faith and confidence I ignored my mom's advice and only applied to this one college.

One in five wasn't very high. I was nervous I might not make it. After countless hours spent pouring over my application, which included five essays, I sent it off covered in prayer. "Lord, please let it be in your will for me to get accepted. I don't know what I'll do if I don't get in."

Several months later, I swung open our large front door and started taking off my jacket in the entryway. My parents quickly came out of their room and told me I had mail. I knew immediately what it was. I snatched it off the table and ran down the stairs into my room. I wanted to open it in private, in case it brought bad news.

I said one last nervous prayer. Then, with trembling hands, I pulled out a single piece of paper which held the fate of the next four years of my life. It read:

> Dear Adriana,
> We are delighted to inform you that your application for enrollment has been approved for the fall semester of 2013.

I gasped. My parents stood at the top of the stairs waiting and praying. I exploded out of my bedroom and bounded up the steps.

"I got in! I got in! Ahhh!"

They wrapped me up in a huge group hug full of excitement and relief. They beamed at me with pride and my mom started raising her hands up and praising the Lord. I was so happy my eyes were watering.

I was going to be trained by world-renowned professors on how to effectively do full-time ministry while also participating in hands-on learning experiences in Chicago. I was going to fall wildly more in love with Jesus, and serve him faithfully every minute I was there. I was going to be in his word every single day, and I was going to make new friends. Everything was going to be amazing. Or so I thought.

Chapter 2: Embarking to Discover

You're rich in love and you're slow to anger. Your name is great and your heart is kind. For all your goodness I will keep on singing, ten thousand reasons for my heart to find.

—Matt Redman and Steve Angrisano

It was a beautiful summer day. I was wearing a yellow short-sleeved Chicago shirt I bought during my college visit last year. I had fashionably chosen to wear my royal blue shorts to complement the yellow and had unfashionably chosen my most comfortable flip flops. My arms and legs were tanned from a summer full of waterskiing and selling cotton candy. My heart was filled with all the eagerness my eighteen-year-old self could possibly possess. It was move-in day.

The line of cars backing up traffic urged us to move quickly as my parents and I unloaded all my bins and bags from the car onto a cart. Once everything was out, my dad went to park the car and my mom and I made our way to my dorm. An upperclassman assisting with new student orientation saw me struggling to push my cart up the ramp and swooped in to help. He was handsome, strong, and friendly—three wonderful qualities. We parted ways after he pushed the cart into the elevator, and I hit the button for the fifth floor.

When the elevator doors opened, my bubbly and spunky resident assistant greeted us enthusiastically. She introduced herself and proudly explained how the hallway and lounge decorations corresponded with our floor theme from Lamentations: God's mercies are new every morning.

I was paired up randomly with another freshman roommate who I had been messaging for the past two months. I knew she had arrived before me, so my heart pounded with suspense and excitement as I walked into our room.

After exchanging pleasantries and an awkward hug she introduced me to her family. My roommate, Josie, stood at five foot seven, her two sisters both at six feet, and her dad at a whopping six foot ten. At barely five foot four, I definitely felt small. They had already lofted both beds to optimize the limited floor space, and I began unpacking and organizing my things. After a couple of hours, it was time for our first session of new student orientation.

I was thrilled about my classes, my professors, my homework assignments, and my new roommate. Turned out we were a wonderful fit both as roommates and friends. I was exhilarated to live in the heart of a major urban setting, especially since it was the direct opposite of my rural hometown of twelve hundred people. I dove right into any and all opportunities to meet new people and make new friends.

* * * * * *

One amazing part of attending a Bible college was each of my peers and I had at least one commonality: a passion to serve Jesus. I was that annoying freshman who talked to nearly everyone I saw. I was so eager to meet all these like-minded brothers and sisters in Christ from all over the country and the world. On my first day in class I ended up sitting next to a girl from Pennsylvania.

"Oh wow, I really love your accent!" I smiled as I secretly chuckled at the way she pronounced the word *water*.

"Thanks! I get that a lot, but the funny thing is I think all you guys are the ones with an accent. Like you have a super thick accent to me actually. Where you from?"

"Minnesota."

"Ohh. Minnie-sohh-ta" She accentuated the long *o* us Minnesotans stereotypically use. She was not the first one to point this out, so maybe I did have an accent after all.

She was a mere five foot two and one hundred twenty pounds soaking wet. Dark brown hair with beautiful light brown highlights flowed down in thick curls about three inches past her shoulders. Gorgeous amber eyes complemented her deeply tanned skin from lifeguarding all summer.

Perfectly shaped and defined eyebrows along with beautiful, dangle earrings spoke to her desire to look good. And she succeeded.

We hit it off right away, and it wasn't long before she became my best friend. I called her Penny, short for Pennsylvania. I introduced her as Penny to my other friends, and ended up accidentally convincing a few of them that was her real name.

As best friends we loved spending time together. Whether we were wandering around a museum, hanging out on a beach by Lake Michigan, or studying for an exam, it was always a fun time. Our friendship quickly became very deep and personal. I was so thankful for her.

One particular evening, we were hanging out at one of our friend's apartments, sitting on the floor. Due to our college's strict furniture policies the floor was a normal place to hang out. Penny and I were horsing around, as friends do, and I was tickling her. Laughing, she rolled onto her back and I positioned myself mostly on top of her and put my hands down towards her sides where she was especially ticklish.

Suddenly, she stopped laughing and her face went white. "Get off, get off, get off." She said it in a stern and panicked whisper so as not to cause a scene.

I immediately moved and whispered back, "What just happened? Are you okay?"

Her eyes spoke before her mouth did. They were full of fear. She shook her head slightly to indicate she did not want to talk about it. "I'll tell you later," she whispered.

We recovered from the intensity of the moment, and continued to hang out with our friends as if nothing happened. As soon as we left, I brought it up. We sat down in the stairwell between floors nine and ten. It was the perfect place for privacy because only one staff member lived on the tenth floor and she always used the elevator. Penny looked like she was about to cry, so I slid right next to her and pulled her close.

She leaned into me with appreciation for my embrace. I patiently waited in the heavy silence as she took a while to select her words. In a hushed tone she muttered, "It's weird because this has never happened before." She paused before slowly continuing, "But when you were, uh, tickling me, well, all of a sudden I had, I had like a really fast, but vivid, like, a flashback or something."

"Whoa. That sounds really scary, looked like it was scary, too. I'm so sorry, Penny. What was the flashback of?"

She confided in me the few fuzzy details she could recall. "It was mostly just a blur, it only lasted like a split second, you know?" She was clearly deeply shaken up by the whole situation.

✳✳ ✳✳ ✳✳ ✳✳

The next day we were working on homework together in my dorm and she brought it up again. I could tell immediately by the tone of her voice this was very serious. "Listen, I've been thinking about last night. And, well, I really want to figure out what happened to me." I nodded for reassurance, and she cautiously elaborated. "I want to try to get that flashback memory to happen again . . . and I thought maybe you could just do what you did yesterday, and we can see if it triggers it?"

I hastily agreed to her plan. She was my best friend after all—I'd do anything for her. And, in my naive stage of life, her request seemed perfectly reasonable to me. If the flashback happened once, surely, we could make it happen again.

Multiple times over the next couple weeks, we replicated the scenario which had triggered the first flashback. Sometimes it worked, and other times it did not. It was awkward for me to do, but I wanted to help.

Ever since the first flashback, Penny was having a terrible time sleeping. She tossed and turned, and woke up startled from nightmares. As two naturally physically affectionate people, we were already in the habit of sporadically sleeping over in each other's beds. However, it was now our new norm so I could comfort her in her restless sleep.

Over time, we discovered her flashbacks were longest and clearest when she was in a partial state of sleep. So, as we fell asleep, I stayed awake a bit longer so I could do something to cause a flashback. It didn't work every time, but almost.

At the end she always startled herself awake. Then she typically relayed what she had seen through shaky breaths and sometimes tears. Eventually, she fell back asleep in my arms. She told me she felt safe and comforted when I held her like that. This created a deep level of intimacy between us—an intimacy most friendships never reach and, arguably, never should.

At first all it took to trigger the flashbacks was placing my hands on her sides and applying pressure to mimic what happened the first time. It was innocent enough. But over time, the touching escalated. I felt deeply uncomfortable about it, but I approached the situation as a task which needed to be accomplished, nothing more.

What we were doing was strange, but it was entirely platonic. She wanted to figure out more details from her flashbacks, and I was just trying to help.

*** *** *** ***

In our eighteen-year-old stupidity we did not find it at all concerning that zero other people were aware of this situation. We believed we could handle this ourselves, and telling others, at least anyone else on campus, was unnecessary.

I had become her closest friend, and she made it clear she did not want anyone else involved. We were on this dicey journey alone. We figured it was just a matter of time until we hit a moment of breakthrough when she felt like she knew enough information about her flashbacks. Once that moment came, we would stop.

However, what had started out as innocent was taking a turn to inappropriate. Our cuddling grew increasingly intense and, gradually, became something I wanted, craved, and looked forward to in a romantic way. I had never felt these feelings towards a woman, and I didn't know what to do.

As my attraction grew, I started having dreams, but mine were far from nightmares. I dreamed of us being together intimately, usually in the same setting we were actually in. These dreams were extremely realistic, so much so I didn't know if what was happening was just in my dreams or in reality.

I do know that we both believed any type of gay romance between us was unacceptable to God and against the Bible's teachings. We knew the path we were on was a recipe for disaster. However, we were not even willing to consider the possibility of getting help.

We believed if we told anyone connected to our college it would lead to us getting kicked out of our school, massive embarrassment, and having to tell our parents. Therefore, instead of bringing our struggle into the light, we allowed things to escalate in secrecy.

Between her flashbacks, her nightmares, my dreams, her dreams, and what was really taking place in our half-awake states, we couldn't figure out what was actually happening. We tried to put the pieces together, but ultimately we didn't know. Then one night, it happened. We started kissing.

I'd dreamed about it before, she had dreamed about it, we had talked about it potentially happening, but this time I *knew* it happened.

I was more awake than asleep, and I knew she was too. Neither of us spoke a word. We both wanted to pretend like it was a groggy, half-awake, dumb decision, but I knew it wasn't. A thrilling rush shot through my whole body. What we were doing was scandalous, and I wanted more. I battled the colliding emotions of joy and dread. Then, immediately afterwards, I was scared. Not because it had happened but because of how much I liked it. I was scared of myself.

I loved kissing her, and I wasn't supposed to. I believed kissing a woman was wrong. I had been taught that from a young age, and I had read it myself in the Bible. *There is no way this is okay . . . right?*

The following evening, she was leaving my room to go hang out with some other friends. As she left, I finally broke the silence we had held about the night before. "Hey, by the way . . . Um, you are a good kisser." My cheeks burned bright red as I sheepishly searched her face. The pause between my stammering sentence and her response felt like a whole minute, but I'm sure it was only a second. I had no clue how she was going to respond, and the anticipation was agonizing.

Will she be mad? Will she agree and flirt back? Will she be sad I am blatantly admitting I am okay with kissing her? Maybe disappointed?

To my delight she smiled back at me with a sparkle in her eyes and flirtatiously said, "You are too."

With that she strolled out of my dorm room. I sat there smiling at the back of the door like an idiot. It was a small interaction, yet we both knew the deeper significance behind what had happened. We had finally spoken out loud what was going on between us, and in the thirteen words we exchanged we said a thousand. We were on the same page. Something was going on more than a friendship, and we both liked it.

But liking it also came with a deep-seated shame. I knew God was not pleased with what we were doing, as this went against how he had designed romantic and sexual relationships. I sensed God's disapproval, but I amplified his disapproval to be far worse than it was. I felt like God hated me for not only having these desires towards a woman, but now for acting on them. I turned his disapproval of my choices into disapproval of me as a person.

How could he ever forgive me? I am a student at a world-renowned Bible school, I go to chapel three times a week, I sing worship songs, I go to church every week, I volunteer at a homeless shelter, I do street evangelism . . . this can't be happening. I am not supposed to let this happen.

I blamed myself. I did not even come close to adequately blaming Satan. *I* needed to get a grip on this, *I* needed to stop, and *I* needed to stop enjoying it. All those "I statements" left me feeling as though I needed to overcome my sin on my own, rather than trusting and relying on God to help me. I was isolated, and worst of all I was isolating myself from God, believing he was too angry with me to want to help.

It was only a matter of time until we brought our affections out from the dark cloak of the night into the light of day. Fully awake and fully aware of what we were doing. I will never forget the date since it is the so-called most romantic day of the year: Valentine's Day.

We were both publicly single and, on our campus, it was normal for single girls to go out on a Valentine's Day date with one or several other girls. So we followed suit, but ours was an actual date.

I planned our entire evening, dressed up nice, and put on my best perfume. I heard her quick knock at my door, and she entered. She had pulled back half of her dark brown hair into an updo, leaving the rest to flow down naturally in thick curls. She wore sparkly dangle earrings, a form-fitting black dress, and two-inch heels. She looked gorgeous.

I grabbed my jacket, but when I turned to leave, I found her leaning back against the door. The passionate look in her warm amber eyes and her beckoning smile made my heart race. I leaned in and kissed her as I dropped my jacket to the ground. *I guess we aren't leaving so fast after all.*

✴ ✴ ✴ ✴ ✴

Over the course of the next five weeks, we stole opportunities to be together behind the backs of everyone we knew. Penny and I were both swept up in the rush of being in a secret gay relationship. Obviously, there were moments when it was fun, and we enjoyed the passion and progression of our relationship. However, most days included moments of deep pain and inner turmoil.

I felt a war raging inside my brain at all times. Unfortunately, this war was eerily similar to my relationship with Shannon. Part of me was so happy. The relationship felt good. I really liked her, and she really liked me, too. We got along extremely well as an item, and the developing romance was thrilling.

But the other part of me firmly believed this was immoral and sinful. Plus, I knew it was a dead-end relationship. I knew I could never marry her, so there was no reason to put ourselves through the process of creating and developing this relationship only to painfully sever our love in the end.

The two sides battled against one another and I was stuck in the middle—in the middle of a war that I created. *It's just love, how could it be wrong? We aren't hurting anyone. Maybe the whole reason Christians are against gay relationships is just based on traditions, society, and culture. Maybe it's okay after all . . .* Thoughts like these fueled one side of the war, but from the other side came thoughts in the form of God's still small voice.

My heavenly Father did not shout at me or condemn me. He did not call me an abomination, nor did he shame me for my choices. He spoke in a calm and gentle voice. I felt I deserved condemnation and shame, but it didn't come. Instead, I felt his sadness for me and with me. Adriana, I am heartbroken by what you are going through. Let me join you on this painful journey. I want to help you. I want to guide you.

His faithfulness and love were impossible for me to comprehend. I fully believed our relationship was not right in his eyes. I believed he had exclusively designed sexual and romantic intimacy for one man and one woman, yet his soft voice assured me my feelings and attractions did not mean something was wrong with me. It was acting upon them that was wrong. I believed with all my heart that I needed his help to put these sinful desires to death and choose honoring and pleasing him over pleasing myself. I did not intend to live my life based on what I wanted to do but based on what God wanted me to do.

However, as the days turned to weeks, I could not figure out how to do that. I desperately tried allowing him to help me stop what we were doing, but I was asking him to take something away from me while I gripped it with a closed fist. I clearly did not actually want his help. He could not remove what I was not truly offering to him.

I cried out to my heavenly Father in despairing prayers. I knew I was sinking deeper and deeper into my sin, but I couldn't seem to stop. I loved being with Penny even though I knew it was wrong. And worse yet, I knew Penny was going through the same inner battle, but if we spoke it out loud then we would have to actually do something to stop. And since deep down neither of us wanted to stop, we chose silence and avoidance.

* * * * * *

The familiar smell of plastics, fabrics, disinfectant, and the slightest hint of fuel exhaust filled my nose as I entered the airplane cabin. I promptly took off my shoes and sat cross-legged in my window seat, grateful my small stature allowed me to sit so comfortably. Penny sat in the seat next to mine and leaned against me. She wore loose sweatpants and a soft gray hoodie, yet she still managed to look incredibly attractive to me. Our flight was bound for Philadelphia, Pennsylvania, and we tightly held hands as our excitement seeped out of all the pores in our bodies.

She had come home with me during Christmas break, and I introduced her to my family and toured her around to proudly show off my state and my roots. Now it was her turn to do the same during our spring break. I had never been to the East Coast and was thrilled to explore with a built-in tour guide, but most of all I was eager to spend a full week of quality time with my secret girlfriend. It was a relief to be far away from our campus so we didn't have to worry about anyone suspecting our romance.

The two-hour flight flew by as we jabbered on every minute of the way. We spent most of the flight trying to decide where to go, what to do, and when to find time to do it all. The first ten days of our break were to be spent in Pennsylvania and the last five days in Indiana visiting a mutual friend.

We hit the ground running and enjoyed several jam-packed days filled with new sights, new people, and new memories. We explored around her small hometown, Philadelphia, New York City, and Ellis Island. I met a variety of family members I had heard so much about and spent nearly every minute of every day with Penny. In the midst of this significant bonding time, we found ourselves pushing our physical intimacy further than before. One morning we finally broached the subject we had been so diligently avoiding.

"What are we doing? This is so wrong," she whispered.

"I know. I know we have to stop, it's just . . . it's just so hard."

With the lid finally off our can of worms we talked on and on about what to do. We cried and mourned together as we acknowledged our mutual feeling that this relationship was unacceptable. We felt guilty for hiding our secret from friends, roommates, and family members, but we also felt too scared to bring our sin out into the light. We wanted to stop being more than friends, but, at that moment, we were not ready to let go of what we had.

It was so difficult to articulate our thoughts and feelings, no wonder we had successfully avoided the topic for so long. We ended our chat in prayer, asking God to communicate with us what we were supposed to do. The morning of our lengthy discussion happened on a Sunday, so after we wrapped up our final thoughts, we headed off to church.

That particular Sunday the pastor graciously preached about sexual sin, brokenness, and confession.

"You must confess not only your sinful actions, but sinful words, and sinful thoughts. The Lord already knows of your sin, but he desires his children to come to him and acknowledge their sins to him. Why? Because he loves you and there is healing to be found in his mercy and forgiveness." The young male pastor with shaggy brown hair and a casual button-up shirt infused tenderness into his deep voice. It was like he was gently pleading with us to listen because he was sharing something of great importance.

I cannot speak for anyone else in the room, but I know he definitely grabbed and maintained the attention of two young women in the crowd. Two women with a strong need to follow through with the heart of his message: draw near to God, even in your sin. I left that worship service feeling convinced the Lord had supernaturally spoken directly to us.

This message brought about a whole new layer to our discussion. A layer that took our entire car ride to hash out. Once we got back to her home, we felt the need to put action to our words and had a time of confession before the Lord, together. We sat in the heaviness of confessing our sins. Repentance is more than being sorry and remorseful, it is a commitment to turn away from sin and turn toward God. Not a slight turn, but a complete 180-degree turn.

God's presence powerfully met us in that moment. Sitting on her bedroom floor in a puddle of tears, he heard our prayers and helped us to make the unbelievably difficult decision to stop being more than friends. It was one of the hardest decisions I had ever made up to that point. Yet God gave me the strength I needed. I wanted to honor God above everything else I wanted in life, including being in a relationship with Penny.

We had essentially just broken up, so we decided we needed someone else to know what had been happening in order to hold us accountable to actually staying broken up. We figured going from friends to more than friends and back again to just friends was not going to be easy. We chose to tell our friend in Indiana: Avery. Our bus was set to leave three days later to visit Avery anyway, so the timing seemed perfect.

Chapter 3: Confiding and Abiding

I will sing through fire and thunder 'cause you are on my side. I
trust you with my life. I know my story, it isn't over. Even against
all odds, you are a faithful God.

—I Am They

Our Megabus pulled up to the curb right on time. It was a cold and
cloudy day, perfect for a long bus ride. Penny and I had spent a considerable portion of the ten-hour journey anxiously processing, planning,
and plotting how to handle the dreaded conversation of confessing to Avery what had been going on between us.

Neither of us wanted to tell her, or anyone for that matter, but we
believed speaking it out loud to a friend was the right move, especially
with the breakup being so fresh. We needed to bring our sin into the light
because we needed support and accountability. However, knowing and believing that was not enough to calm our fears.

Penny was extra leery of telling our friend Avery. She thought it was
too soon and tried to convince me to wait and tell someone else on campus
once the dust had settled. To her credit, this plan could entrap us if the conversation went poorly, because we couldn't leave. We were stuck together
for five days no matter what, and that was a risk I figured we just had to
take.

We stretched out our sore and cramped bodies as we searched for our
friend in the small crowd gathered to pick up loved ones. Avery spotted us
first, trotted over, and wrapped us up in big hugs.

"Wow! I can't believe you guys are here in Indiana! I can't wait to show
you guys around my neck of the woods!" We matched her enthusiasm and

exchanged joyful remarks about being together. She guided us to her 2002 white Pontiac Grand Am which clearly showed signs of its age and use. We loaded our bags into her trunk next to jumper cables, a windshield scraper, a tow strap, and a backup jug of oil.

Avery lived out in the country on a gravel road, so our activities could be described as "hick." We went mudding on her family's four-wheelers, shot at clay pigeons, and went horseback riding. In a streak of eighteen-year-old-level wisdom we drove seventy miles per hour on the gravel roads while taking turns standing up through the sunroof. It was a blast. Lucky for us, none of our faces were marred by flying pieces of gravel. But in the midst of the fun, Penny and I were trying to find a moment that felt right to drop our story on our unsuspecting friend.

* * * * * *

It was sixty-five degrees and sunny, perfect spring weather for a hike. We donned some athletic shorts and shirts, complete with baseball caps and tennis shoes. Venturing through the woods, Penny and I soon began exchanging nonverbal and whispered communication as to whether or not this was the right opportunity.

A fallen tree became a pit stop to catch our breath and enjoy our surroundings. The lakeshore was just twenty yards off to our left and the sunlight sparkled and bounced on the surface of the water. Birds, squirrels, and bunnies joined us during our little break as they rustled around in the brush. The timing felt like it couldn't get much better, so with great trepidation I awkwardly initiated the topic that had been secretly hanging over our heads like a dark cloud.

I cleared my throat. "So, listen . . . we, uh, well, we have something important we wanted to talk to you about." I stammered nervously, "We haven't told anyone about this, um, but we wanted to tell you because we need help and accountability. We want to shed light on, um, on what we've been doing because we want to stop." I was trying to preface it carefully so we did not completely blindside her. Naturally though, it also increased the awkwardness.

After an uneasy pause I proceeded to share an abbreviated version of events. I talked nearly as fast as I could, since I was so ashamed to be admitting it all out loud. I figured the faster I spoke the sooner I could be done talking.

The part I did not brush over quickly was the ending. "So after that powerful encounter with God and time of confession we really have turned away from our sin. We know it's wrong, and we have stopped everything already and just need accountability to make sure that continues so we don't fall back into our old ways. And that's why we wanted to tell you, so maybe you could help hold us accountable."

No wave of relief came from having finally shed light on the truth. Instead, my stomach flip-flopped in knots as I waited for her response, petrified. Time felt like it was in slow motion.

"You guys know this is homosexuality, right?" Her voice sounded full of judgment and even disgust. We looked down at the ground, in shame, and both nodded.

That was her opening response, and when it comes to any type of vulnerable confession like this, a person's initial response carries a significant amount of power. The power to comfort, build up, or encourage, or the power to tear down, embarrass, and hurt.

She continued, "Well, I mean I can try to keep you guys accountable or whatever, but at the end of the day you guys might need to, like, not be friends anymore."

I protested on behalf of us both. "We really believe we can still be friends *and* overcome this sin. We have already stopped being with each other inappropriately." Her face clearly indicated she was neither convinced nor impressed with my response.

She countered, "I don't know, something to consider, I guess. God might want you two to stop being friends because of all this."

Dozens of words were communicated in a single glance between me and Penny. Her eyes told me, "See! I told you it was too soon! Now this whole trip is ruined because we told her."

An uncomfortable tension filled the air. We had put the truth out there, and her response hurt us both, but at the same time I couldn't blame her for it. She was shocked, she was only nineteen, and she was woefully ill-prepared to lovingly encourage us in our unique situation. After more awkward comments were exchanged, we all stiffly got off the log and walked back towards her car.

She eventually broke the tense silence. "You guys might not want to hear this, but I don't think it's a good idea that you guys are sharing a bed. I think we should change our sleeping arrangements around."

I vehemently opposed, "No. That's not necessary at all."

Penny added, "We aren't going to do anything bad. We promise."

We were particularly surprised to hear her say this considering the bed we were sharing was in the same room as the bed she was sleeping in. Implying she believed we were willing to still mess around even with her in the room.

She continued, "Well what about changing clothes in front of each other? Maybe you guys should start doing that in separate rooms."

We tried to assure her that no logistical elements needed to change because we had already successfully stopped our behavior. To be fair, it had only been a week. We hadn't had much time to prove ourselves, so she wasn't instilled with much confidence.

* * * * * *

"See. I told you we should've waited," Penny whispered angrily to me a few hours later.

Three and a half days stood between this awkward conversation and our return to campus. Those days were tense. Avery brought up changing our sleeping arrangements again, this time asking if one of us was willing to sleep on the couch. On top of still feeling this was totally unnecessary, it also would raise suspicions and questions from her parents and siblings. Questions we did not want to answer.

She begrudgingly relented. Her distrust in us could not have been more apparent. We felt deeply ashamed. Since Avery was the first person we had told, we were particularly sensitive.

Avery was confused how we had allowed this to escalate to this point, especially if we both believed it was wrong. Why didn't we get help right away? Knowing it went against our school's code of conduct, did we even consider telling someone from the school about what had been happening?

These were legitimate questions, but they only made us feel even worse. Plus, they pointed to one of my biggest fears: being kicked out of college. I figured if any staff or student leaders found out about what we had done we would be expelled. Worse yet, then I'd have to tell my family, and that was my greatest fear of all.

I shuddered at the thought of telling my parents their upstanding and trustworthy Christian daughter had gone off to Bible college and messed around with another girl. My mind ran through dozens of versions of that conversation, and zero of them were positive.

Avery's reaction was unsettling to me. I planned to never tell anyone else about this, since it seemed I'd only be setting myself up for more shame and embarrassment. The rest of our time in Indiana went quite smoothly, all things considered. We stuck to our plans as normal. The only major change was Avery's hesitancy to let us leave her sight, but we felt this was somewhat justified. Our honest confession and Avery's response to it had left our friendship in an uneasy state.

Her parents dropped all of us off in Richmond and we boarded another Megabus, this one bound for Chicago. Six hours later, after arriving back "home," we quickly returned to our daily lives and routines. Nearly no change resulted from having confided in Avery. In some ways she tried to be there for us, but she was a bit too disturbed by our secret to really hold us accountable and help us in the ways we had hoped.

* * * * * * *

Our negative experience of opening up to Avery solidified our shared view that we shouldn't tell anyone else, so we didn't. We struggled alone in the complicated breakup of a relationship that we partially did not want to end. We tried to remain close friends. We still slept over in each other's rooms, we hung out on campus and off campus, and we desperately tried to be together without *being together.*

We wisely adjusted the quantity and quality of time spent together. We were careful to not be alone together too much, we set up strict physical boundaries, and prayed for our friendship to become platonic once again.

Going back to a platonic friendship after crossing the lines we had crossed was complicated and immensely difficult. As time passed, it was clear I was fighting harder for our friendship to stay intact than Penny was, and the reason became evident by the end of that school year. She started dating a guy, Stephen.

I listened to her talk about Stephen in that cute giddy way girls talk about their crushes. They started going on dates several times a week, and spending lots of time together. All the while, I watched as my closest friend and former girlfriend began getting all her relational needs met by another.

I felt abandoned, heartbroken, and, for the first time in my life, jealous. I wanted to be the one she wanted, and I felt replaced. I had to stand idly by while she moved on, and it stung.

Summer arrived in all its glory as the spring semester came to an end. We returned to our respective home states and slowly lost contact until I eventually faded out of her life. There was no big falling out, no confrontation, not even a goodbye. I do admit, however, that the gradual nature of the end of our relationship made the healing process easier. Bit by bit I let go of my hopes of being best friends again.

Several years later, she and Stephen got married. Unsurprisingly, I was not invited to the wedding. But I was happy for them, especially for her, even though I was still struggling to get past the damage done to my heart after falling for her. Something had shifted deep within myself, but I either didn't know it or I knew and didn't want to believe it. I thought I could just move on like she had. I could just fall in love with a godly man and live happily ever after.

Chapter 4: Shalom Y'all

I'm not afraid to show you my weakness. My failures and flaws,
Lord, you've seen them all and you still call me friend.

—Elevation Worship and Brandon Lake

The dry desert air slapped my face and filled my lungs. Taxis, shuttles, and buses awaited tired travelers and the drivers called out loudly to anyone passing by. I had arrived alone in Tel Aviv, Israel, for my three-month study abroad semester. I did not fly with the rest of the group because I had only purchased a one-way ticket. I intended to find a ministry to partner with for an additional three months after the study abroad finished.

The study abroad was to last three months, January through March, but my summer job did not start until June. So, rather than sit at home for three months I wanted to use my time to serve the Lord. The rest of the thirty-person group were set to land late that night. Thankfully, my plan was approved by one of the professors in charge, and he had thoroughly prepared me to find my way to the hotel.

I avoided eye contact with the very loud and aggressive-sounding drivers and tried my best to act like I knew exactly what I was doing. My professor's warning ran through my mind: "This is not the place where you want to look lost or in need of help, especially not as a young American woman. These guys are just trying to make a living, but they can sniff out the opportunity to double their prices. You cannot under any circumstances go in a taxi—you need to find a shuttle."

I assertively made my way towards the shuttles and eventually located the large white vans I was looking for. After double-checking this was the right company, I asked for the price to be brought to Hotel Yehuda in Jerusalem.

"Yehuda? I'm not sure." My pleasantly helpful driver replied and gestured at my paper implying I should elaborate.

"It's on Chaim E. Kolitz Road. Here . . . um, it's right here." I pointed at the words on my paper and he immediately understood. I blamed my poor communication on my American accent. With a price agreed upon, I handed him the appropriate number of shekels, and he graciously loaded my heavy suitcase into the back. I climbed into the shuttle and found a seat among the other passengers. We waited in the hot van until every seat was filled.

When I checked into the hotel, I discovered there was another student from my college who had arrived early, too. His name was Cade, and we already knew each other relatively well. Neither of us had dinner plans, so we ventured off to a local grocery store and shared a loaf of bread together. Nothing else, just bread.

After our unexciting dinner, we slowly walked back to the hotel, trying to kill time. A task that was not difficult for two chatty people. We settled into our hotel rooms, and the rest of the group arrived in the middle of the night.

In no time at all, our group became very close. Which is unsurprising considering we were together nearly 24/7. We ate every meal together at the exquisite hotel buffet, we were in class together for at least four hours every day, we frequently worked on homework together, we played games, and we went off on adventures in Jerusalem.

I was privileged to room with a couple of girls I already knew, Tamika and Sunset. Sunset was already my friend, and I gave her that nickname early in our friendship due to her bright red hair. Each hotel room came with two single beds and one terribly uncomfortable cot. We, along with most other girl rooms, decided to push the two single beds together and create one large bed for all of us to share. Being the most physically affectionate of the three of us, I happily agreed to sleep in the middle.

During the first week we spent substantial amounts of time chatting and getting to know each other better. Our conversations progressively became more personal. One late evening, we were sitting on our mega-bed, cross-legged in our pajamas, chatting away about our lives. I asked, "Do either of you have anything you are afraid to tell other people about?"

Alarms sounded off in my brain as soon as the words left my lips. *Why on earth did you ask them that?! You know once they are done answering they are going to say, "So how about you?" Genius. What are you gonna do then? I can't believe you asked that . . .*

✳︎ ✳︎ ✳︎ ✳︎ ✳︎

Even though my question was on topic, I truly believe this was a rare moment in life when God literally spoke through me. My mouth was moving, the words were forming, but I did not actually intend to ask that question. It just spilled out of my mouth, seemingly beyond my control.

Inevitably, the moment I dreaded came. "So how about you?" Sunset asked.

My stomach churned and sweat had already accumulated in my armpits and on my forehead. I knew I should tell them. Somewhere, deep down inside, a piece of me even wanted to tell them. But I was so deeply ashamed and afraid. As we sat together on our large combo-bed, time seemed to freeze.

I should tell them.

No, what if it makes things awkward between us? We do have to share this room together for three more months.

But they are great people, and incredibly kind and understanding. Surely, they are good people to tell.

I don't know, there's just no way to know how they will react. What if they think I am gross, or make me tell someone else? Like one of the profs in charge of the trip or something.

This internal struggle displayed itself externally in my facial and body expressions. Plus, my silence gave me away. I obviously had an answer.

"Adriana, you don't have to tell us. But if you are willing to share with us, we will be happy to listen." Tamika's words soothed my anxious thoughts. Sunset echoed the sentiment. Then they did something seemingly small, but deeply needed: they graciously and patiently waited.

Their willingness to wait spoke louder than any words. The silence told me they loved and cared for me and would wait as long as it took. I knew I wanted to tell them, so I desperately tried to form the words, but I felt physically inhibited. I took a deep breath. "I . . ." That's all that came out as I hung my head in shame. I tried again. "Last year, I . . ." I clenched my jaw. My breathing got heavy. I was sweating all over by this point, and shaking, too.

This went on for several minutes. I wanted to spill my guts and just lay it all out there, but I was terrified to bring my sin into the light again. I hated how this went the first time around with Avery, and I did not want a repeat of that.

I tried to talk, but then stopped. I didn't know what to say. I didn't know how to say it. They were patient and gentle, and broke the silence. "Adriana, it seems like you really have something on your heart to say. You can do this. We know you can." Sunset briefly put her hand on top of my own to assure my clearly shaken up spirit.

Just take a deep breath. Come on. They were not going to give up waiting, and continued to encourage and reassure me, until eventually I spit it out. I stammered and fumbled my way through my story of my secret gay relationship with Penny. I shared about how it started, how it escalated, and, ultimately, how it ended.

They hugged me. "Thank you so much for sharing that with us. That was brave." Sunset continued, "Clearly it was a very difficult and scary thing for you to share, so we are honored that you trusted us with it."

Their noncondemning, compassionate response astonished me. I really had thought I'd never try to tell anyone else. The wave of relief that rushed over me was equally as intense as the fear I felt just minutes prior.

"Adriana, we do not view you any different because of what you told us. And nothing needs to change in our interactions unless *you* say they do."

I had no idea how much holding in my story had been weighing on me until I spoke it out loud again. I felt the weight lift off my shoulders. This felt like a moment of victory, like it was all over. It was something that happened, it was wrong, and now it was done. I didn't have to dwell on it or think about it anymore. I believed it was simply a piece of my past, but I was wrong.

✻ ✻ ✻ ✻ ✻

One girl in the group, Maria, was what one might call a firecracker. She had straight blonde hair which stopped at her shoulders. She was my height with multiple ear and face piercings and an adorable splatter of freckles on her face.

Her fiery, outspoken, and blunt personality was similar to my own. So we were not instant friends. It took some getting used to one another to realize our similar traits need not drive us apart but could unite us together. She soon became, hands down, my closest friend in the group.

After just one week, a few people came up with the idea to start doing testimony nights. Every Sunday night two people volunteered to share their testimony, each one lasting thirty to forty minutes. Since there was so much time to fill, people generally shared their entire life stories, and I loved every minute of it. It was so interesting and bonding to hear people's stories, and there was an element of healing in the air as people had the unique opportunity to walk through their life journeys step by step.

Despite faithfully attending each week, I had zero interest in sharing my story. I was not even remotely prepared to bring my story into the light on such a grand scale. And, to me, it seemed dishonest to give a censored version of my life story when all my friends and peers were being completely vulnerable and authentic. However, from the very first testimony night, I heard God's still small voice calling me to step out in faith. I WANT YOU TO SHARE YOUR STORY. TO SHARE YOUR WHOLE STORY.

No way! I am not anywhere near ready to share my story. It was hard enough to summon the courage to tell Sunset and Tamika, not to mention telling like twenty-five people. Some of which are guys, by the way! No way. I'm not doing it.

I loved my classmates, but the issue was that after sharing I would continue to be around this same group of people every day until the end of the trip. If I could just share my story and never see them again, that would be easier. Instead, whether they reacted positively or negatively, I was stuck with them. This was a main reason for trying to ignore God's prompting.

I thoroughly explained my reasons to God, which is ironic considering he can read my mind. But he, ever so patiently and lovingly, shot down each of them over the course of about six weeks. Despite my protests, his call on my heart was unwavering. It turns out once you know God is the one calling you to do something, or not do something, disputing is fruitless. By the end of those six weeks, I lost the argument.

Before sharing my story with everyone, I wanted to tell Maria first. She was my closest friend in the group, so I felt she deserved to hear it from me personally. Plus, we were physically affectionate people who regularly rubbed each other's backs, exchanged long hugs, sat in each other's laps, and sometimes slept in the same bed. So she had extra reason to be informed of my past relationship.

Thankfully, despite all our physical affection, I did not feel any physical attraction towards her. I proudly relished in my ability to be so affectionate but not have any romantic desires.

* * * * * * *

Five of us sat down a dead-end hallway in the hotel. A dozen red-cushioned couches were piled in several stacks in what appeared to be a makeshift storage area. We pushed two against a wall and worked on our homework assignments together. It was past midnight, which was typical for our group of chronic procrastinators. Our homework took us twice as long to do together, but it was far more enjoyable than doing it alone.

The rest of the group went off to bed one by one, until it was only me and Maria. This was an ideal circumstance to tell her my story. I thought I was ready to share with her, but my sweat, churning stomach, and pounding heart said otherwise. I feared after telling her she would be concerned about my potential attractions and distance herself from me.

I set aside my assignment and leaned forward. She picked up the non-verbal cue and sweetly asked, "Hey, what's up?" I didn't say anything.

"You okay?" She reached out and put her hand on my arm. I became a stammering flustered mess again, much like when I told my roommates. As I struggled to form the words, she assured me, "Adriana, there's nothing you can tell me that will make me love you any less."

It was as if she read my mind. Thanks to traversing this road before, I got it off my chest much faster this time, and, like my roommates, she was patient, kind, and compassionate.

After pouring out my heart I added, "I promise you I am not concerned about my friendship with you. It's not like that with you, and I am so excited to be able to love you and be affectionate towards you without having it be unhealthy or wrong. But, if now knowing my story, you have concerns and want to change the dynamic between us . . . like, if you don't want to share a bed with me anymore, or anything like that, then I totally understand."

She grabbed both of my hands and held them in her own, pulling slightly to cause me to angle my body to face her. She looked me dead in the eyes as she spoke with a serious tone. "No. If you say nothing has to change, then nothing has to change. End of story, as far as I am concerned."

"Really?" Her complete confidence in me was a pleasant surprise. I realized this "bomb" was maybe more of a small grenade. Maybe my appearance and style gave me away a little bit. The new information I presented did not need to impact the closeness of our friendship. To say I was relieved is a massive understatement. She asked if she could pray for me, and I gladly accepted.

After finishing our homework, we gathered up our things and made our way through the long hallways toward our rooms.

"You sleeping in your room tonight or mine?" she asked in the same way she had habitually asked over a dozen times before. Nothing had changed, just like she said. She trusted me, and believed in me. Smiling wide, I said, her room, and fell asleep cuddled up close to her.

✻ ✻ ✻ ✻ ✻ ✻

I arrived at the classroom fifteen minutes early and the chairs were already set up in the standard large circle. My fellow peers and friends started filing in. I was so nervous I thought I might actually throw up. My testimony night partner, Deion, was a calm, cool, and collected kind of guy. I was grateful for his tranquil demeanor which starkly contrasted mine. He graciously agreed to let me go first.

I had requested Tamika, Sunset, and Maria sit in three different parts of the circle. That way, when I looked up for eye contact, I'd only look at them. A group of about twenty-five had gathered and one of the testimony night leaders called for everyone's attention. And just like that, the floor was mine. I swallowed hard.

I can do this. I can do this. God's soothing still small voice spoke to my heart and assured me everything would be fine. This group loved me and they were not going to shame me for my story. Feeling a supernatural sense of peace, I took a deep breath and started from the beginning.

After describing my family and childhood, I launched into my relationship history. I started with my high school boyfriend, Shannon. Then, with much trepidation, I shared about my relationship with Penny and my attraction towards women. I talked at a respectable pace, but I couldn't cover up the quiver in my voice.

After someone finished their testimony, the entire group surrounded them for a time of prayer. I pulled my chair into the center of the circle and then everyone came and stood or knelt close to me—close enough so nearly everyone could reach and put a hand on me for the prayer. I felt hands on my back, neck, legs, shoulders, arms, and even my feet.

They did a waterfall prayer. One person opened in prayer, then every single person prayed in unison until it grew quiet again, and finally one person closed in prayer. It was loud and chaotic yet concurrently beautiful and tender. Since they had just heard my entire testimony, their prayers were shockingly specific.

The chorus of voices enveloped me. I basked in the intensity of having that many people pray for me at once. I understood why it was called a waterfall prayer, because it felt like their prayers were washing over me. Refreshing and renewing me deep inside. It was awesome.

I received several heartfelt hugs after the prayer. I was no longer afraid, anxious, or ashamed. I was calm and proud of myself. It was a massive stride in vulnerability.

Through the love and affirmation of my friends, God taught me that sharing my story did not mean people would judge me, think differently of me, be nervous around me, or make assumptions about me. I looked around at the faces of my peers and I felt profound contentment.

* * * * * *

Maria and I were spending time together in the evening on the same red-cushioned couches in the storage area and got to talking about the five love languages. According to Gary Chapman, author of *The Five Love Languages*, they are: physical touch, words of affirmation, receiving gifts, quality time, and acts of service.[1] Our top love language was the same: physical touch. Casually she asked, "What is your favorite form of physical touch?"

"When someone softly caresses the insides of my forearms." I showed her what I meant with my own arm.

"Really? Like this?" she asked as she reached over and gently caressed one of my forearms.

I smiled. "Yep, exactly. What about you?"

She hesitated in telling me, so I prodded a little. "C'mon . . . You can tell me. What is it?"

---

1. Chapman, *Five Love Languages*.

She blushed and caved to my pressure. "Well it's a little unique, I guess. But I absolutely love it when someone touches the inside of my hip bone right here." She demonstrated for me as her right thumb slid just slightly under her pants and underwear to the inside of her hip bone. She was right, it was unique.

That night as we fell asleep, we exchanged those acts of physical touch. Since we had just been talking about it, I felt this was normal interaction. But in reality my mind was mixed up about what was physically appropriate between friends due to my relationship with Penny. Penny and I had crossed so many lines friends do not cross that I now struggled to know what was acceptable and what was off limits. This was particularly difficult to navigate with such a physically affectionate friend.

Shortly after falling asleep, Maria woke up panicking from a nightmare. Her panic was impossible to contain, so she jumped out of bed and ran into the bathroom to avoid waking up her roommate. I hastily followed and held her in my arms as she cried on the bathroom floor.

I tried to provide calm reassurance, but she was really shaken up. Eventually, she slumped over into my arms, totally exhausted, and nearly fell asleep. I got her back into bed and she quickly fell asleep.

During class the next day, she had very curt interactions with me, so I knew something was bothering her. We hung back once class was dismissed, and she quietly asked, "Did anything unusual happen last night?"

"Well you had like a panic attack shortly after you fell asleep. You said it was because of a nightmare." I described the whole ordeal in detail, and that was it. We never spoke of that night again, until a year later. I had no idea how much that night would impact my life.

I readily admit that what I did was over the line for what is permissible between friends. However, to this day, I do not consider it to be morally wrong. It was unwise and unnecessary but not immoral. Furthermore, this act was never repeated, nor anything similar to it. We were two young girls who were touchy-feely and made some dumb decisions.

Maria and I loved each other as friends and nothing more. However, this messy moment in our friendship showed me I had a lot more personal work to do in recovering from my past relationship with a woman. I needed to be more careful than the average friend. I likely needed to set up boundaries with friends from the get go, for their protection and my own.

I had a lot to learn, and I had just learned the hard way. I didn't want to have to treat myself differently just because of my past, but I realized it was necessary in order to maintain God-honoring and healthy friendships with my female friends. This was a difficult pill for me to swallow, but I was committed to improving. I knew for certain I did not want what happened with Penny to repeat itself—ever again.

I knew God wanted me to be careful. Not because he is a God who wants to punish me for my stupid behavior or my sin, but because he wants what is best for me and wants to protect me as his daughter. He wanted my heart to heal from the past, and he wanted to shield me from hurting it again in the future. Any shame or hatred I thought he had toward me was entirely my own projection. He loved me and cared for me. I believed that with all my heart.

Chapter 5: Roller Coaster Ride

What heights of love, what depths of peace, when fears are stilled, when strivings cease. My comforter, my all in all. Here in the love of Christ I stand.

—Stuart Townend and Keith Getty

"Well, hey there, Sandy! Did you leave any beach behind for other people to enjoy?" I teasingly asked in a thick Midwestern accent to my new roommate when she walked through our door with legs covered in sand.

She always loved when I used that accent to make my jokes, and cackled loudly. I began laughing too just because of how hard she was laughing.

"Sandy!" She squealed with delight and laughed even harder. And just like that, her nickname was born.

When I find a nickname I like, I aggressively commit to it. In fact, my level of commitment has reached the point that I have, more than once, forgotten a close friend's real name. My new roommate felt left out and had been begging me to come up with a nickname for weeks, but I can't force the creation of a good nickname—it has to happen naturally.

From that day forward, I called her Sandy. Sometimes I lengthened it to Sand-meister or shortened it to just Sand. She enjoyed her nickname so much she began to introduce herself as Sandy. Eventually, there were a considerable number of our peers who believed that was her real name.

Sandy had specifically reached out to me to see if I wanted to live with her for her senior year in hopes of finally having a positive roommate experience. We were friends, but not close friends. She was confident we were going to get along splendidly. However, I quickly discovered the common denominator to her bad roommate experiences . . . was her.

She was a burdensome roommate. She struggled with mental health difficulties which led to an unhealthy and chaotic life, a life that was now intricately wrapped up with my own. But it was not all bad. Underneath the turmoil and unpredictability of living with her was a tender friendship. There were moments of uncontrollable laughter, late night chats, and deep heart-to-hearts.

As a caring roommate, I found one particular part of her life concerning: her friendship with a married man named Todd. I felt as though how often and at what times of day they were texting and calling was inappropriate. I expressed my concerns and, over time, she came to agree.

Together we discussed what healthy boundaries looked like for them. Finally, she worked up the courage to call him and instill these new boundaries. She said it was awkward, but he seemed to receive it well. Their adjustment to a new normal went smoothly.

However, in the wake of losing her close connection with Todd she felt lonely. I started to worry about how she was going to bounce back, but, to my surprise, about a week later, she shared some exciting news with me.

"So this is way outside my comfort zone, but I reached out to this guy I used to have a crush on in high school, Diego, and now we've been talking quite a bit!" she informed me with giddy excitement.

"Wow! That *is* outside your comfort zone! What made you decide to reach out to him?"

"Well, it's kinda lame, but I actually had a dream about him randomly. So after that dream I looked him up on Facebook and found out he's still super cute."

"What? Let me see!" She happily obliged and we scrolled through a bunch of Diego's pictures, giggling and chattering on like girls do when talking about a boy.

A couple weeks later I was met with more exciting information. "Guess what?"

"What?"

"Diego wants to hang out with me when I go home for fall break!" She squealed with joy, and I was so happy to see her happy. The timing seemed sent from the Lord above. One difficult relationship removed from her life and an exciting new one starting.

After fall break, Sandy eagerly gave me another update.

"We are officially a couple. Like boyfriend–girlfriend!"

I was ecstatic for her, and gleefully listened as she told me about his family, his job, his interests, and of course their romantic date over fall break. As expected, he began calling and texting her regularly. Every day she talked with him for well over an hour—and sometimes late into the night.

Our friendship was becoming increasingly close, so I accepted her invitation to join her family for Thanksgiving. I enjoyed meeting her family and exploring her hometown area, especially being in a state I'd never been to before.

Throughout Thanksgiving break I was hankering to finally meet this boyfriend, but we slowly ran out of time to meet up with him. Whenever the chance presented itself, he was unavailable, or when he was available, we were not.

I was disappointed, but nevertheless, we started our drive back to Chicago. As we drove, we got into a deep heart-to-heart. She spent three hours straight sharing hard and heavy moments of her life with me.

Nearing our familiar Windy City, we stopped at a gas station, and she broke down in tears. I put my arm around her and held her as she wept. She told me she had never told anyone most of those stories before and she felt overwhelmed having finally gotten them off her chest. I was honored she trusted me enough to be so vulnerable.

Later that night, we were discussing her boyfriend, and I said we should pray for their relationship. We already had a roommate routine of praying every night together before going to sleep, so this suggestion was not out of the ordinary. But she grew deeply distraught and eventually started sobbing in a heap on the floor. I had no clue what had caused such a reaction, so I sat down next to her to try to figure it out. It took quite a bit of coaxing before she choked out, "I lied to you."

She did not have a boyfriend. She never had a boyfriend. The guy she was pretending to date was a real person, with a real Facebook account, but the truth was she had not spoken to him since high school. My mind was reeling with this earth-shattering information. As I tried to digest that she had been telling me a massive lie the obvious question dawned on me. "Wait a minute. So who has been texting and calling you all the time then?"

I was too dumbfounded to sound accusatory. I was genuinely asking. Her face dropped and I arrived at the answer on my own during the excruciatingly long pause that followed. Finally, she confessed. It was Todd. They had never stopped talking after all.

✻ ✻ ✻ ✻ ✻ ✻

Through shaking breaths and tears streaming down her bright red cheeks, she claimed it was all his idea. When she told him I was concerned about their friendship, he concocted this plan to get me off their case. She had remained silent because she was terrified I would be angry and her confession would ruin our friendship.

Surprisingly, I was not angry. I was shocked, confused, and hurt. I felt like an idiot for having fallen victim to a massive act of manipulation. But most of all, I felt sad for her. I was sorry this had been happening all along and she felt helpless to put it to an end, and that she endured it in total isolation.

Several nights later, when I had come to terms with what had happened, I did feel betrayed. She had lied through her teeth, for weeks. However, despite the betrayal, her bravery in admitting the truth brought us closer together than ever before. I was the only person who knew about what had been happening, the only one holding her accountable to making it stop, and the only person she truly trusted.

Somehow, I did not recognize this as a problem. The writing on the walls should have been crystal clear to me, especially considering what happened with Penny. Being the only person to know something as significant as this was unwise and unhealthy. I should've known better.

A major reason I fell into this trap, again, is that it feels so good to feel needed. I loved having friends be vulnerable with me and share things they had never shared with anyone else. I felt important to be the only one carrying a heavy burden with a friend.

In my immaturity, I did not believe we needed to involve anyone else. We could handle this ourselves. But now I know that is simply an appealing lie to believe. We are not designed to depend on only one person; everyone needs a strong support system. This holds true regardless of age, gender, marital status, or faith.

However, I do think scenarios like this can be particularly dangerous among female youth and young adults. For some reason that demographic is more prone to depending on one another in unhealthy ways. We are prone to finding a best friend and pouring out our hearts on serious topics, and then being too afraid or ashamed to tell anyone else. I've heard it time and time again.

This dysfunctional dynamic can manifest itself in the form of codependency. According to Dr. Jonathan Becker, an associate professor of clinical psychiatry at Vanderbilt University, "Codependency can be defined as any relationship in which two people become so invested in each other that they can't function independently anymore."[1]

I believe the messiness of codependency and the variety of ways it transpires in relationships makes it hard to determine if and when it is happening. Dr. Becker goes on to explain how one's mood, happiness, and identity become defined by the other person.

Of all the unique and complicated relationships I found myself in over the course of my life, the one I know without a doubt crossed into codependency was with Sandy. We were far too wrapped up in each other's lives to maintain a healthy separation of our persons.

For example, if she was having a bad day that meant I was having a bad day too. She relied on me and needed me in ways I could never satisfy, and yet I craved being needed by her. My distorted sense of identity caused me to feel overly responsible for Sandy's actions and emotions to the point that I neglected my own needs.

However, at the time, I saw nothing wrong with our friendship. I truly believed I was being a good friend and doing the right thing. I thought I was being helpful and loving. Really I was jumping into deep water to save a drowning friend only to drown with her. There were plenty of trusted people we could've confided in, but Sandy was not interested. She was scared of what people might think of her and was too embarrassed to confide in anyone besides me.

As time went on, we began keeping more and more topics to ourselves. One of those was her struggle with fits of rage. Oftentimes I did not know why she was angry, including when I was bearing the brunt of her anger. It was not unusual for Sandy to become so frustrated that she would throw items around the room. She never threw objects directly at me, but they were often thrown in my general direction.

She yelled loudly both to me and at me. I am sure she would've happily slammed our door, but the hinge mechanics did not allow for it. Instead,

---

1. Gilbert, "Do You Have."

she stormed out of the room and slammed her hands on the back of our door. Then she slammed her hands along the wall next to the door, knowing my desk touches that wall. Finally, she made it to the stairwell door and slammed that door.

One time we were getting ready to watch a movie with some friends, and a seemingly minor disagreement ensued over the popcorn. She furiously stormed out of the kitchen and into our room.

When I walked in to talk to her about what had happened, she slapped me across my face. I was stunned speechless and walked out of the room. She came after me apologizing. She gave me a hug and tried to explain herself. I forgave her, mostly because it was the easiest way to avoid further conflict.

At times I was afraid to enter my own room. I didn't know if she was depressed, furious, or pleasant. This unpredictable roller coaster of emotions was taking a toll on me. It also grew increasingly difficult for me to navigate how my choices and actions factored into her emotional state, but I knew her emotional state directly determined mine.

If she was in a good mood and having a good day then I did too. If she was somber and sad, I felt like I should be too. And if she was angry and raging, how could I possibly have a good day? This issue of dependency ultimately led to unhealthy intimacy. She came home with me for the first half of Christmas break, and there our unhealthiness swelled.

※ ※ ※ ※ ※

My parents and sister observed how Sandy and I interacted and saw red flags. They pointed out how I acted differently around her, but I was immediately defensive. They expressed concern over how she seemed to want to control me and the way I used my time. I scorned their concerns. *She is not controlling me, that's ridiculous.*

Little did I know, I was being wrapped tighter and tighter around her finger. She controlled how I used my time, the way I interacted with people, my opinions of other people, and who I was friends with. However, I was ignorantly blind to all of this. Not just blind but quick to excuse and justify her behavior.

I knew she was in a tough place in her life and her faith. I wanted to be gracious and compassionate. Meanwhile I mistakenly allowed our friendship to grow increasingly unhealthy. Sandy was not just controlling and manipulative, she was also depending on me far more than was right or fair to either of us.

She allowed me to believe she needed me in order to survive—she even verbalized this belief. On rare occasions if I was not behaving how she desired, she threatened me, "If you don't cancel your plans, there's a chance I'll just kill myself tonight then." She used my empathy and fear against me. I wanted to do anything I could to help her with her mental health struggles, even to the detriment of my own mental health.

Some nights I spent hours trying to convince her not to kill herself. Eventually I became so exhausted I couldn't talk anymore. However, if I tried to sleep, she would leave the room expecting me to chase after her. A couple of times I chose to sleep on the floor in front of our door just to prevent her from leaving. I was desperate to catch some sleep, and I felt this was the only way. She aggressively protested against me sleeping there, but eventually she'd give up and go to sleep.

Sandy's use of control and manipulation were designed to be subtle. She never outright said what I could or couldn't do, but she swayed my decision making with passive comments of what she wanted. Some of it even came down to tone or nonverbal cues. "Oh, you are going to work on homework with Josie this afternoon?" This seemingly simple question could be asked in a manner that I knew she didn't want me to do homework with Josie, prompting me to investigate. "Yeah, why?"

"Oh, nothing." Her body language, demeanor, eye contact, facial expressions, and tone all worked in tandem to elicit the reaction she wanted.

"Do you not want me to or something?" She then typically used something emotional to make me feel guilty, maybe claiming to feel particularly sad or lonely. She conveyed that if I truly cared about her then I would cancel my plans. How I spent my time, who I spent it with, and when I spent time with them began to fall under her control.

My parents and sister were not the only ones to voice their concerns, but I pushed away any notion there was something wrong. I believed since I was the only one she really trusted that I was the only one who really knew her and everyone else was arriving at false conclusions based on what they didn't understand. Only I could truly grasp her pain and the way she was because of it. Before I realized it, my friendship with Sandy was causing a direct strain on nearly all of my other friendships. But yet again, I was blind.

Spending large amounts of consecutive time together over Christmas break had lent itself toward some unhealthy physical intimacy. One morning, I was putting on my snowboarding gear, which includes a bandana over my face for wind protection. She sat on my bed waiting for me to get ready and out of nowhere I went up and kissed her on the lips through the bandana. We giggled about it like it was no big deal, as if it was normal. Only a few weeks later, we actually kissed.

It kind of just happened. We were sitting on her bed, which was normal at the time because our dorm room only had space for one comfy chair. Since we both didn't fit on the chair and our beds were set up as a bunk bed and we typically hung out on her lower bunk. One flirty comment and interaction led to another. Afterwards we again acted like it was normal, but we knew it wasn't.

✳✳✳ ✳✳ ✳✳ ✳✳

For nearly two weeks we had been gathering food whenever we could in an effort to stock up for our spring break road trip. We collected apples, bananas, oranges, granola bars, and chips from the student dining hall. Our dorm floor lounge table, affectionately called "the altar," was a place people left items they did not want, and then said items were snatched up on a first-come, first-served basis. The days before spring break the altar received a lot of traffic as people got rid of food that would go bad if left behind. Thus, the altar greatly benefitted our stocking up efforts.

The night before we left, we stayed up until three in the morning planning out the details of the trip. The parks, the hiking trails, the little pit stops along the way, and all the logistics. We planned to put the backseat of Sandy's little Ford Focus down flat and sleep with our heads in the trunk. It was not the most comfortable arrangement, but we were going to make it work. We loaded up the car with blankets, pillows, food, clothes, and towels.

I was desperately looking forward to the chance to escape the chaos that my life had become during that semester. I wanted to get away and not think about anything but our adventures. We were southern bound: Chicago to Florida.

After three days full of pit stops, hiking, and lots of driving, we finally arrived and joined the rest of our mission trip group. Thirteen of us college students had decided to give up half of our spring break to serve those in need in Florida. For one week we worked at a rehabilitation facility for adults recovering from substance abuse. We participated in their programing and connected with the residents. The girls on the trip worked with the women and the guys with the men. Since much of our ministry centered around relational opportunities, being sociable was necessary to be effective.

Sandy was glued to my side. I kept encouraging her to branch out and build her own relationships but she said I was so much better at conversing and connecting with others that she preferred to tag along with whatever I was doing. I found this annoying but tried not to let it show. I was flattered by her consistent compliments on my ability to build meaningful relation-ships in such a short time frame.

After the mission trip concluded, we spent seven days making our way up the East Coast to Philadelphia then turned straight west back to Chicago. During this trip, the whole social and relational interactions, or lack thereof on her part, became a point of contention.

She disclosed, "Honestly, I am kind of embarrassed that I'm not as social and outgoing as you."

"Oh, that's no reason to be embarrassed. We are just different, that's all. It's not a bad thing or a good thing, you just have a different personality than me."

"Well, it's not just being outgoing and social. You are just so good at connecting with people. Like, you ask the right questions and everyone loves talking to you and opening up with you, it's really amazing actually. When we would show up to the women's house, they always lit up when they saw you there, and I was just kind of, like, just there in the background."

Her explanation did not sound like a compliment—it felt like she was jealous of me. It seemed like she was irritated that we weren't the same in this way. I tried to assure her that others did not see it that way and that she had nothing to be upset about. She didn't seem satisfied, but we dropped it.

Silence ensued until I finally couldn't drive any further. We found a parking lot with low enough lighting to sleep but public enough that we felt safe. We set up for the night in the back of the car, and our exhausted bodies allowed us to quickly drift off to sleep.

⁎⁎ ⁎⁎ ⁎⁎ ⁎⁎

Due to Sandy's mental health struggles, our trip was filled with high highs and low lows. Since we were spending nearly every moment of every day together, we of course had moments of frustration and annoyance. However, the intensity of her frustration was not normal.

One evening, Sandy was driving late into the night. She became so furious with me that she slammed on the brakes as hard as possible, sending us to a screeching halt. We were in the middle of nowhere, in the dark, on the side of the road. She started screaming at me at the top of her lungs until she eventually exhausted herself.

She stormed out of the car, slamming the door behind her. She started walking back in the direction we had come. I sat in the passenger seat shocked by what had just unfolded. I was afraid of her. I was scared she might hurt me and scared she might hurt herself. My spring break was not the escape I was hoping for; it was the opposite. I was trapped.

I was stuck on this road trip with her. Unless one of us literally abandoned the other on the side of the road, which started to feel like an entertainable option, there was no choice but to keep pressing forward. I debated whether the safest choice was to get out and chase after her or wait in the car and hope she would come back on her own.

All I wanted was to get to where we had decided to stop for the night and sleep, hoping the morning would bring a better mood to my travel companion. I waited several minutes before I finally got out and yelled, "Sandy! Where are you even going to go?"

"What do you care?!" she snarled back.

I started walking towards her. "Just come back, please. We gotta keep driving. It's getting late." I felt like I was pleading, but I tried to make my voice sound strong and sure. She muttered something in response, but I had already turned around. I decided after the shock, and even pain, of her slamming the brakes it would be best if I were driving. I sat in the driver's seat and waited.

Ten minutes went by before she came back and plopped down in the passenger seat without saying a word. Grateful to be on the road again, we drove over thirty miles without speaking. I didn't want to risk setting her off again. Eventually she turned the radio off and began to apologize. However, her apologies no longer felt sincere. Apologies mean a lot less when there are no actions to back up the words.

This normal pattern of chaos then apologizing for the chaos was so familiar that forgiveness was my default. It was still the easiest way to respond. If I just forgave her, then the conversation ended and we didn't have to hash out what had happened.

Discussions on why a moment of rage happened and ideas on how to prevent it in the future were long and unpredictable. I was usually so emotionally exhausted I didn't want to talk about it anymore anyway. Plus, her apologies were just empty words to me now.

* * * * * * *

We liked the atmosphere of "roughing it." Our diet of PB&J sandwiches, crackers, fruit, and granola bars left our bodies in survival mode. Especially when paired with significant miles of hiking and walking each day. We were exhausted, to say the least, and the back of the car was far from a restful night of sleep.

On top of all this, we had such a jam-packed itinerary we were typically getting to sleep around 11:30 p.m. and waking up before sunrise. These factors contributed to my lowered self-control, even lower than usual. I passively allowed the physical component of our relationship to progress. I almost never turned away her advances. Most of this happened in the back of her car, late at night.

One day, a song came on the radio that we had never heard before. We liked how it sounded and turned it up. Lyrics about late-night driving with the windows down, going places you can't pronounce, and doing things you've dreamed of doing seemed very fitting for our trip. Before getting through the whole song, we said this could be "our song."

Then the lyrics took a romantic turn. Lyrics about doing things you know you shouldn't do, causing trouble in hotel rooms, and having secret rendezvous. We threw each other several side glances. Sadly, these lyrics were also fitting for our trip. Our flirtatious silence spoke volumes and we finally acknowledged there was something happening between us.

Since we were Christian women who believed the Bible teaches sexual intimacy is designed exclusively for marriage between one man and one woman, we had recurring discussions on how to create and maintain physical boundaries. Like my relationship with Penny, we both felt terrible about the decisions we were making. We were cyclically discussing the problem and trying to come up with ways to stop, but then we would fall into our desires and temptations time and time again.

I felt far worse about the whole relationship than she did. At times it seemed like she was waiting and hoping I would come to the conclusion that it was not a big deal. Love is love, right? I could be with a woman if I wanted to be. It's true, I could. But then I'd have to live with the reality that I was directly disobeying God and what he wanted for me and expected of me. And I just couldn't do that.

I wanted to obey God. I wanted to follow in his ways and live in a way that honored and pleased him. In fact, that was my heart's single greatest desire. The very purpose of my life is to serve God and glorify his name. I knew I was falling short of that purpose in times like these, but that did not change my drive to seek him and live for him. That drive was still there.

Toward the end of our trip, we decided to find a church service that fit into our schedule. We did not care how bad we looked or smelled because it was the house of God, and he didn't care. We parked in the church parking lot for the night, and settled into our "bed." We prayed together as we did every night and peacefully drifted off to sleep.

The next morning, we woke up well before our alarm and one thing led to another, and we allowed ourselves to escalate our intimacy further than we had ever before. On a Sunday morning. In the parking lot of the church we were about to walk into. Which is exactly what we did.

We grabbed our toiletries and got ready for the day in the church bathroom. Then we attended the worship service. I could not believe myself. It felt like a nightmare, but I knew it was really happening.

As I stood there singing along to the worship songs, I was overcome with guilt and remorse. I repented of my sins, and prayed. *God, please help me. Please give me the strength to resist my fleshly desires. I am so sorry God, I don't want to be stuck in this sin anymore. Please, please help me.*

I started weeping as quietly as I could, trying not to draw attention to myself. Sandy noticed and reached for my hand, but I pulled away. I was so disgusted with myself I could hardly stand it. I imagine not a soul in that church could've guessed what was weighing on the hearts of the two weary travelers sitting in the back row.

In the heaviness of this moment, I felt God's tender love for me. The worship team was singing one of my favorite songs. My throat was closed too tight to sing, so I somberly let the words sink in. Tears crept to the corners of my eyes and began to slide down my cheeks. I quickly wiped them away with my sleeve.

A woman in her mid-forties with straight blonde hair wearing a beautiful lavender dress was leading the worship song. The instrumentation continued as she spoke out with a slight southern accent, "We are going to sing that chorus again, but this time I want you each to make it your own.

Declare over yourself the things to which you are no longer a slave. To fear, to anxiety, to depression, to sickness, to sin, to heartache. Whatever it is for you. And maybe it is something you no longer *want* to be a slave to, but you are struggling against at this moment. That's okay. God knows. Sing it out. And listen to the declarations around you as we sing: We. Are. No. Longer. Slaves."

Some scattered "Yes, Lords" and "Amens" rang out in the congregation. With all my heart and soul, I sang out, "I'm no longer a slave to my sin, I'm no longer a slave to my desires, I am a child of God."

I wish I could say this powerful worship experience allowed me to turn everything around. That I stopped being intimate with Sandy, and never looked back. But sadly, I cannot. I don't know how long I lasted before caving to her advances again, but it happened. And it kept happening. We got back to our Bible college, and nothing changed. In fact, it only got worse.

Chapter 6: It's Complicated

It's love so undeniable I can hardly speak. . . . You're a good, good Father. It's who you are. And I'm loved by you. Its who I am.

—Chris Tomlin

Throughout our spring break trip, I had a cloud hanging over my head and a pit in my stomach reminding me of my dread about returning to campus. I had found myself in quite the predicament, stemming from my friendship with Maria. We had remained friends throughout the spring and summer following our study abroad trip in Israel. During the summer, she went through some hard situations, and showed up in the fall with a broken heart.

After the first few weeks, she began to isolate. She pushed away all of her friends, including me. It was very difficult to make plans with her, and when we did find a limited window of time to spend together, she did not want to open up about anything personal. Eventually she started ignoring my calls and texts altogether. I did not understand why this was happening, and I was hurt.

It felt like she did not care about me at all and was unfazed by our meaningful friendship fizzling away. We had been through a lot of amazing experiences together, and I considered her one of my closest friends. Now it seemed our friendship was a one-way street. I cared about her, I reached out, I wanted to spend time together, but none of that seemed to matter to her.

One night, to my surprise, she initiated hanging out with me. She planned to be in a study room until late into the night working on home-work with some friends and asked if I wanted to join. I happily accepted, but as I watched her interact with her other friends, I grew increasingly hurt by our unreciprocated and superficial friendship. I concluded that she could laugh and be her "normal self" around these other friends but not around me.

Half past midnight she packed up her things and went around the table saying good night and hugging everyone. When she got to me, I hardly even looked up from my laptop and mumbled, "Good night."

The awkwardness of the moment hung in the air. The rest of her friends couldn't help but observe our unpleasant interaction. She gave a little shrug, said good night, and left. Feeling guilty, I texted her a couple minutes later, "I am sorry I didn't hug you. I regret it now. I hope everything is okay. I am here for you if you ever need anything from me. Good night, Maria."

"Come outside." The response came in less than a minute. It was October 6th in Chicago, not exactly a nice evening for a chat. Nevertheless, I made my way out to the plaza where I found her sitting on a bench.

"Listen, I'm just going to be really blunt and honest with you. I am really struggling right now, like in this season of life." I was so grateful she was finally sharing vulnerable things with me.

She explained briefly some of what was going on in her life. "So because of all this I just am not in a place where I have the emotional capacity or the energy to be a good friend to you. I'm sorry, I just don't. I'm not going to be able to reciprocate the kind of friendship you want with me. My life is just a mess right now. If you want to come into the mess with me, you can, but on the condition that you don't try to clean up the mess. You can sit in the messiness with me knowing that I cannot be a good friend to you."

I listened intently as she continued, "I definitely understand if you aren't interested in doing that or in being my friend right now. I won't hold it against you in the slightest." It was not an emotional discussion. She spoke plainly and simply as she presented the facts of the situation.

I responded without hesitation, "Maria, I will happily enter your mess. And I understand you don't want me to do anything to clean it up. I will just love you and care for you the best I can with zero expectation of anything from you in return."

* * * * * *

After our conversation, I texted her, "I'm like super excited to love you right now! Like I just wanna go buy you a pop tart and scratch your back or something!" I was relieved that her lack of reciprocation had nothing to do with me personally, and I was ready to accept the challenge of loving my friend who couldn't love me very well in return.

For the rest of that semester, I put an incredible amount of time and effort into supporting and caring for her. I bought her candy, brought coffee to class for her, even classes I didn't have with her, I left her encouraging notes, I prayed for her all the time, and sometimes sent her those prayers via text. I persistently checked in to see if she was doing okay or needed anything.

I knew there was an important distinction between Maria being a private person versus isolating herself. I was committed to trying to keep her from isolating in unhealthy ways. I know I did not do this perfectly, and I may have even been overbearing at times in my eagerness to show her love and support.

Our friendship was erratic. Sometimes she was genuinely happy to see me and grateful for the ways I was trying to love and support her. But other times she brushed me off, sometimes seemingly annoyed by my presence or my acts of kindness. Some weeks I was lucky if she would offer me a ten-minute slot between classes to see her, but other weeks we spent hours and hours together. Somewhere along the line, I started sending her texts starting with "Dear D," and ending with "Love, J."

I didn't tell her why, but after a few of those texts she guessed it. I was referencing a profoundly deep friendship between Jonathan and David which is recorded in the book of First Samuel of the Bible. Jonathan was the son of the first king of Israel, and David was the young shepherd boy who killed Goliath and later became the top leader of Israel's armies.[1]

I explained in a text.

> I know I have no right to compare myself to Jonathan, and maybe I shouldn't even. And I realize I will never love you with a love like Jonathan's, but I am striving for that kind of love. I am not Jonathan, but I want to love more like he loved, and not just with you but with my life in general. I believe David and Jonathan are such a picture of how friends can deeply love one another while consistently keeping their friendship godly, pure, and glorifying to God.

The last sentence meant a lot to me because of my past relationships. I wanted to love deeply and intimately, like David and Jonathan, but not

1. 1 Sam 18:1.

cross the line into being inappropriate or sinful. Their friendship gave me hope and dared me to believe I did not need to be afraid of emotional and relational intimacy with my friends.

She replied, "That's really sweet and it's an incredible life to strive for." With that I started sending her the "Dear D" texts nearly every night. Texts full of prayers, encouragement, affirmations, reflections, and compliments. Each one ended with:

> I am here for you always.
> Love,
> J

* * * * * * *

I scanned our campus coffee shop looking for Maria. She was wearing a fuzzy black jacket and stylish black and white patterned pants. Her dark brown eyes looked up from her phone and met mine. I pulled out the wooden chair across from her at a small table for two. We were meeting up one last time to say goodbye before she left to go study abroad in France for the spring semester. An undeniable tension filled the air as we exchanged pleasantries.

Toward the end of fall semester and over Christmas break things felt off between us. I was hoping to get to the bottom of it so we could leave off on good terms before her study abroad. The hissing sounds from the espresso machine and clanging around of the coffee shop workers filled the background as we started talking. It quickly became apparent there was a notable shift in our friendship.

"Sometimes it felt like you were way too intense about checking in on me. I know you had good intentions, but wondering about you and what you would do next started to become its own origin of stress in my life. You texted me all the time, and I knew if I didn't answer you'd follow up within a few hours. And sometimes I just needed a day to myself." Maria flatly explained her perspective.

I was surprised and sad to hear her say all this. I had tried so hard to support her during a rocky season and now I found out, at times, it was not even wanted. *What a waste of my time. If she didn't appreciate what I was doing, she should've told me.*

I replied with the same flat tone she was using. As if we were emotionlessly exchanging observations on the past semester. "I'm sorry to hear you felt that way. I didn't mean to be a cause of stress in your life, especially with everything else you have going on. I was just trying to help. And after our conversation in the plaza, I knew that you wouldn't be able to reciprocate a normal friendship with me, which I totally respected. But I guess I felt super hurt when it seemed like you were able to reciprocate friendships with some of your other friends. So, then, it kinda seems like I just wasn't worth the effort of friendship with you but others were."

"Well, in all honesty, when I told you all that in the plaza, I never expected you to actually accept the challenge of being my friend. I thought for sure it would scare you off and you would give up on our friendship and leave me alone. I actually not only expected that to happen, but I was kind of hoping for it. And instead, you like doubled down on being my friend."

"What?! Well why didn't you just say that in the first place then? You are one of the most blunt and straightforward people I know; it shouldn't have been hard to just be honest with me." So much for the emotionless exchange of observations. I felt betrayed, but was still doing all I could not to draw attention to us from fellow students sitting nearby.

"I know. I should have just been more up-front, but I didn't realize how I felt until afterwards. For what it is worth, I am sorry. I know this semester has not been easy on you, and I know I am part of the reason for that. I have interacted with you in a way that is confusing and unpredictable, and, for that, I do apologize." I nodded and accepted her apology.

She continued, "So, speaking of being blunt and honest, I just want to be really straightforward with my expectations moving forward. I really want to be present with the people I am with during my study abroad in France. I don't really want to stay in touch at all while I am there. I just think messaging you and having video calls would be too distracting for me."

"No problem. If you don't want me to stay in touch with you, then I won't." I was not too saddened by her request because staying in touch with her would have required effort on my end and I was exhausted from trying to be her friend. Plus, like she had just said, her responses to my efforts were unpredictable, confusing, and hurtful. The idea of having a semester-long break from one another was a welcomed respite. We awkwardly wrapped up our conversation, and that was it. She left.

✻ ✻ ✻ ✻ ✻

February 8th. A day seared into my memory. I had not spoken to Maria in almost a month, and I was well into the groove of the new semester. I was peacefully sitting in my ministry internship class one morning when my phone vibrated. It was a text from Maria. "I'm on campus and I need to talk to you asap. When are you available today?"

She's on campus?! What the heck! I wonder what happened. Something terrible, probably. Maybe one of her family members passed away or something, or maybe she got hurt in France and had to come back. My stomach was churning, and I couldn't concentrate on my professor's teaching at all. I was worried sick. After finding out she could meet me right away in the commons, I left class early.

I ran down the stairs and then speed-walked my way toward the commons. I found her sitting in a booth, fashionably dressed like usual, but looking distressed. I slid into the seat across from her, and when I looked up I could see traces of fear in her eyes.

"Hey, I came as fast as I could. What's going on?" I was out of breath and my voice was quavering.

"Well, while I was in France, I was absolutely miserable the whole time. I called a friend of mine to chat, and I ended up just talking about Chicago and how much I missed being here on campus. Every time he asked me about France, I couldn't think of anything positive to say. So, finally, he asked why I was even there in the first place, and that's when it hit me. I realized I went to France to get away from you." She paused, allowing me a brief moment to try to digest her jarring words.

"After realizing that was the main reason I left, I decided I should come back and try to see if it wasn't too late to join some classes here on campus. So I dropped out of study abroad and got on a plane back here. I scheduled a meeting with the dean of students to talk to him about if I could enter classes this late in the semester. But he wanted to know why I dropped out of study abroad, and, well, I didn't mean to tell him all this. It really was not my intention."

Her prefaces put me even more on edge. "But, well, he started asking questions. Like really direct and pointed questions. He, uh, well he asked about you and about our friendship, and then I ended up telling him about that night in Israel."

She was acting extremely intense, but I wasn't even sure of what she was talking about. "What night in Israel?"

She explained, as if should've known, but I had totally forgotten about that night.[2] "Anyways, after I told him about that night, he said I needed to file a case against you, otherwise he would have to do it himself. I'm sorry, I didn't plan to tell him about any of that. He just asked a lot of really direct questions, and I couldn't get around them. And it sounded like the case being filed by me would be better for you in the long run, so that's what I did. I promise I did not go to his office planning to do this, I didn't even want to, but, like I said, those were the two options he gave me."

My brow furrowed as I looked down at the table. My mouth was dry, my mind was spinning, my heart was pounding. I was in shock. Finally, I choked out, "Okay, so what happens now? You filed a case against me? What does that even mean?"

"Well, it's not a criminal case. So it will stay 'in-house', like with our campus security and admin," she explained calmly, clearly not shaken up by the situation. "I don't know very much about the process, but I think they will have to meet with you to ask you questions and stuff like that. I don't know how it will start, but I just wanted you to hear about it from me first. I didn't want you to be blindsided by this whole thing, and I'm sure campus security will be the ones contacting you next."

I nodded to indicate my understanding because I couldn't get out any words. She continued, "Also, when I met with the dean I found out it is too late for me to register for classes on campus, but he said I had permission to audit classes. So I've already found some off-campus housing and will be here to audit several classes. If we cross paths, I would like to kindly ask you not to interact with me in any way. It would be better for me and my mental health if we had no contact. I hope you understand."

I didn't understand. This was too much information being divulged all at once. However, if she wanted no contact from me, so be it. I wasn't going to argue or ask for more explanation.

I tried to appear calm but inside I was in pure panic mode. We exchanged a dry and brief goodbye, and parted ways.

2. See page 38.

59

Chapter 7: Haunted by a Mistake

He is jealous for me. Loves like a hurricane, I am a tree bending beneath the weight of his wind and mercy. Oh, how he loves us.

—David Crowder Band

I felt like the ground had been ripped out from underneath me. I hurried down the hallway avoiding eye contact with anyone around me and praying no one I knew saw me. I leapt up the five flights of stairs to my dorm floor. I was too afraid to go to my own room because I was convinced campus security officers were out to get me. I thought they were going to come escort me to some kind of detaining room until all of this was resolved.

I went to a friend's room who I knew had class for the next couple hours. I slumped down onto the floor, hugged my knees close to my chest, and rested my head on them. I had never been this anxious before in my life. I was covered in sweat. It felt as if my whole world, my whole life, was unraveling.

What have I done? Did I do something wrong? What is going to happen to me now? Am I going to get arrested or something? I catastrophized the situation as my mind ran through a rampage of worst-case scenarios, all of which terrified me. I was too scared to cry. Part of me just wanted to pack a bag and run away.

Over the next hour, I slowly calmed down. I realized the best thing for me to do was to get up and get on with the rest of my day, so that is exactly what I did. Then I did it again the next day, and the one after that. Eventually, eighteen days went by and not a single person contacted me in any way about Maria's case. I figured Maria had blown everything out of proportion. *Maybe this whole thing will just go away, maybe no one will ever even contact me about it.*

But on the eighteenth day, I received an email from an administrator asking for a good time in my schedule to come in for an investigation meeting. After corresponding regarding some possible days and times, we decided to push it off until after spring break which was just around the corner. Hence, the cloud hanging over my head and the pit in my stomach throughout all of spring break.

The interrogation meeting happened in a small conference room with a campus security officer and the administrator who had emailed me. They asked dozens of questions and listened to my side of the story. Several questions were uncomfortable ones, specifically on the nature of my relationship with Maria and the night in question. The meeting was stressful but tolerable.

As we wrapped up, the administrator stated, "We will potentially be getting in touch with you either via email or another in-person meeting." I left feeling further confirmation that this was not as big of a deal as I had originally thought. It seemed there was a possibility they wouldn't even get in touch with me again. I was relieved.

It was only later that I discovered either this administrator misplaced the word "potentially" or I misheard her. Apparently, she meant to say, "We will be getting in touch with you and it will potentially be by email or another in-person meeting." Which is a big difference.

☆☆ ☆☆ ☆☆ ☆☆

I returned to life as normal. Unfortunately, my "normal" was chaotic. I was over the maximum amount of credits allowed per semester due to a loophole I found in taking one online course and a full load of in-person classes. I was involved in five weekly ministries, I worked part-time at Chili's Grill & Bar, and I attended church every Sunday. I was chronically exhausted from this schedule and a lack of sleep.

I was also emotionally exhausted. The most troublesome aspect of my life was my relationship with my roommate. She became jealous of any amount of my very limited free time that I spent with anyone besides her. Since my days were so incredibly full, I often reached out to friends to see if they could grab a meal in the cafeteria with me. For several of my friends this had turned into a weekly routine.

In what I now believe was an effort to further control my time and who I spent it with, she came up with a reason as to why I needed to start eating all my meals with her. I believed her reason, even though it might've been made up. My other friendships suffered as I canceled my mealtime plans with them.

Often people in toxic relationships do not realize they are being controlled and manipulated; this was true for me. If anyone tried to express concern, I defended her. I brushed aside their concerns, believing they simply didn't understand the whole picture like I did. *She isn't controlling me. She just needs my help. They don't get it.*

In the midst of the control and manipulation our ability to maintain healthy physical boundaries started deteriorating. We went through waves of remorse and regret, but then we slipped right back into the same patterns of behavior. We agreed upon and enforced strict boundaries. At a certain point, we even agreed to zero physical contact for a week.

It seemed like none of our boundaries worked: no sleeping in the same bed, no physical contact, no cuddling, no holding hands. We went through so many boundaries it became difficult to keep track. I felt trapped in an endless cycle of guilt, repentance, pep talks, establishing new boundaries, failure, and back to guilt again. Over and over and over.

I wanted God to help me break the cycle and act in a way that was honoring to him. But part of me also wanted to continue in my sin. It felt good to be wanted, it felt good to be kissed, and it was exciting to see how far we would allow our relationship to progress.

I avoided deep moments of prayer because I did not want to hear that still small voice beckoning for me to change my ways and honor him. But God is everywhere, including dwelling inside of me,[1] so it is impossible to hide from him and his voice. At church, at my ministries, during class, in conversations with friends, in the bathroom, doing an assignment, in all times and places, he was there. I was perpetually afraid he was angry with me, so most of the time I did all I could to ignore him.

Think about that. A Bible college student actively involved in ministry is admitting she did her best to ignore God in order to continue in her sin. It's quite embarrassing when phrased that way, but it is true. That is exactly what I was doing. And I know I am not alone in this. Each person faces unique struggles, and each Christian faces unique temptations.

1. 1 John 4:20.

Many followers of Jesus face a similar scenario simply with a different set of sins. Maybe it's pride, or poor stewardship of resources, or drunkenness, or lying, or stealing. The point is, regardless of what may make people attempt to run from God, we will fail. I failed.

I couldn't flee from his presence, I couldn't run from his arms, I couldn't hide from his love for me. And neither can you. His love is everywhere. He is for me, he is with me, and he is all around me. In my darkest moments, in my wandering away, and in my deliberate rebellion he still loved me and still pursued me.

I knew this was true because any moment I allowed myself to sit and be with him, to actually welcome his presence, I was only ever met with tenderness and love. It moved me to tears, every single time. It was easier to avoid these moments than it was to have to confront the real issue at hand: my relationship with Sandy was negatively impacting my relationship with God. Severely.

Of course, my relationship with Sandy was not all bad. We had some wonderful dates and times together. Often we stayed up late into the night having heart-to-hearts. Those heart-to-hearts proved to be helpful during the tumultuous process of the case Maria filed against me.

Sandy was always there for me. She was eager to hear about the situation, my pain, and my fears. It was comforting to have someone with me every step of the journey. In fact, she was the first and only person who knew about what was happening for over two months.

I had fallen into the unhealthy dynamic of obtaining support from only one person on a significant issue. A dynamic which I had been on the receiving side of for both Penny and Sandy. Deep down I knew it was not wise, but I did not want my other friends knowing about this mess in my life. It was embarrassing, and talking about it was awkward and complicated. I was particularly grateful for Sandy's love and support when I finally heard back from the administrator.

It had been three weeks since I met with them. Three full weeks of returning to life as usual. Then the administrator sent me an email requesting another in-person meeting.

* * * * * *

The room was small with soundproof glass on all sides. There was one round table and four chairs circling it. I never knew this room existed; in fact, I had never been in this part of campus before. We were on the administration floor, and this room was right in the middle. It was a nerve-racking situation, but, considering the lengthy process to arrive at this moment, I felt calm. *Okay, worst case scenario is they require me to call my parents and tell them what happened.*

I took my seat across from the same two people who had conducted my investigation meeting. I casually reciprocated their greetings. The woman took the lead on the meeting. She was in her thirties with dark brown hair and tender eyes. She wore a simple professional blouse and black pants.

She slid a piece of paper in front of me to follow along as they outlined my required actions. *Required actions, huh? I guess that's a nicer way of saying consequences.* I glanced down at it but quickly returned eye contact with her as she thoroughly worked through each of my required actions.

For over five minutes she outlined several, simple required actions, such as no contact with Maria and required counseling for a year. But then she dropped a bomb on me. "Lastly, you are dismissed from school for one academic year, effective immediately."

"What?!" I nearly shouted. I frantically searched the paper in front of me to confirm she had really just said that.

She continued softly, "You will be given forty-eight hours to pack up your belongings and leave campus. Unless you choose to file an appeal."

My focus locked onto her words as she explained the logistics and grounds for an appeal. I spoke with a quavering voice. "I want to appeal this decision on the grounds that the consequence given is grossly disproportionate to the act committed."

The tears I had been desperately fighting flowed down my face. I covered my mouth to try to physically suppress the sobs which were accompanying my tears. The campus security officer pushed a box of tissues across the table as I swallowed hard and tried with moderate success to collect myself.

Since I was appealing the decision, they invited the dean of students into our meeting. He thoroughly described an intense appeals process for me to follow. A group of nine people would hear a verbal appeal from me along with two character witnesses of my choosing. I was to approve of these nine people and voice any concerns of bias. The process sounded very fair, giving me ample opportunity to explain my perspective and ask for reconsideration.

During the next two weeks, I poured myself into preparing my appeal statement. It was my new number one priority. I stopped submitting assignments and even missed some of my weekly ministries. I met with and helped my two character witnesses prepare as well. The hearing date and time were set, and I approved the nine people set to determine my fate.

That morning my stomach churned like never before. I had to skip breakfast just to keep from vomiting. I picked out one of my nicest outfits, trying to look professional. I anxiously waited for 11:00 a.m. to come around.

Late that morning, while I was in class, I received an email from the dean of students. The meeting was canceled. He had informed me of the incorrect appeals process, and his email didn't even include an apology for his terrible mistake. Not only did he give me false information when it was his job to oversee appeals, he gave me false hope. I was not sad, I was furious.

* * * * * * *

I wanted to storm into the dean's office, but you need an appointment in order to see him. Plus, his secretary surely would've stopped me from barging in. I resorted to sending him a strongly worded email. Then I read over the new process he had outlined in his email.

Instead of nine people deciding my appeal it was only three, and my approval of them was not taken into consideration. They would receive my appeal statement in writing, and there were no character witnesses. No apologies, no sympathy, and seemingly no regard for how this sudden change of plans impacted me.

My ability to stay and finish the semester was dangling in the air entirely based upon a decision from three strangers. I tried to press on with my school work as usual, but it was extremely distracting to have this hanging over my head. *What is even the point in doing my assignments if I am just going to get kicked out anyway?*

The only fruit that came from my strongly worded email is that I was allowed to submit the appeal statement I had already written despite it being six pages over the new maximum length. Other than that, I was given no modifications. I submitted my statement and waited in excruciating anticipation.

They refused to tell me the day and time they were meeting to discuss my appeal. As I anxiously waited, the semester was quickly drawing to an end. *What am I going to do if they deny my appeal? The semester is almost done. Is my work this semester going to end up being all for nothing? Why is this taking so long?*

Then a passage of Scripture popped into my mind. Maybe it was God's still small voice or maybe it was just my own brain summoning part of a verse I knew I needed to hear, Psalm 46:10: "Be still and know that I am God."

I didn't know how to do that. I trusted God and believed with all my heart that he is able to work all things for my good.[2] I knew he loved me and had not abandoned me. Yet, every single day, I was afraid and anxious. *Be still and know? What does that even mean?*

The appeal decision was set to come to me via email. Therefore, every time I checked my email, I had to make sure I was physically and mentally in the right space to receive the news. Preferably alone in my room, but that was not always possible.

The waiting and checking were agonizing. I had no idea how to "be still" when I was white-knuckling it through each day. I believe being still is a mindset. One that involves complete and total surrender to God and his will. Be still, be quiet, be tranquil, be at peace, be calm. I was none of these things, and I did not know how to become them.

I was a nervous wreck, and I now know it was, at least partially, because I did not fully trust God or surrender to his will. I had no control over my situation and the impact it would have upon my future. Control is something I liked to have, as most people do, and I was a mess without it.

As more and more days went by, I grew hopeful they wouldn't reach their decision until the semester was over. Those hopes were dashed when I had made it incredibly close to the end. It was the Thursday of the last week of class before finals week: May 5th. My appeal was denied.

My hands rose to my face on instinct at the horrible news. My devastation physically impacted me. I was dizzy and nauseous. It felt like someone had sucker punched me in the gut. I was alone in my room, and I desperately wanted physical comfort.

Two close friends of mine were roommates who lived just down the hall. Their nicknames are Jammie and Grammie, and they both knew about the case against me and my appeal. I lightly knocked on their door and found Grammie sitting on her bed studying.

---

2. Romans 8:28.

Grammie immediately could tell something was wrong and dropped what she was doing as I plopped down on the bed next to her. Knowing I was anxiously awaiting a decision on my appeal led Grammie to the natural conclusion I had received bad news, but she didn't ask. She gave me a safe space to deal with my emotions any way I wanted.

I played the song "Cry" by Kelly Clarkson, and, in suit with the lyrics, the floodgates behind my eyes gave way and released a torrent of tears and sobs. Grammie tenderly comforted me while I cried in her lap. Eventually I felt the need to verbalize what had happened and choked out, "They denied it, Grammie. They denied my appeal." Hearing myself say those words made me cry even harder.

"I'm so sorry, Adriana," Grammie answered while rubbing my back. She was the perfect person to tell first. Her almost motherly empathy and kindness soothed my heart. No other words were exchanged for nearly ten minutes. Words fell short at a time like this anyway.

Her silent presence and physical comfort were exactly what I needed in that fragile moment. She offered to skip her next class to stay with me, but now I just wanted to get off campus. I wanted to be outside and be alone. I borrowed a friend's longboard, and rode the familiar half-mile journey to my favorite Lake Michigan beach.

* * * * * *

I found a spot where the waves of Lake Michigan, one of the Great Lakes, loudly crashed onto rocks and boulders by the shore. I sat down and wept as I prayed, "God, why is this happening? I just don't understand. Aggh, I am so mad. Why did the whole thing have to take so long? I am practically done with the semester. And what happens now? What am I going to do?"

On and on I prayed. At certain points I was yelling. I fluctuated from sad and confused to cold and bitter. I was not listening for God's still small voice. I was too frustrated to listen. Instead, I just held my head in my hands and cried.

Strangers passed by me in an unending flow of bikers, walkers, and runners. But none of them could hear me because the waves and wind drowned out my voice. I sat there until I was completely exhausted. I hurt so deeply I could hardly wrap my mind around the complexities of my emotions. Finally, I made myself get up and continue longboarding. I stopped again at the end of a pier and sat down.

This spot blatantly contrasted my last one. Here the water was so deep the water silently rose and fell in a steady rhythm. It looked like the lake was breathing in and out. I filled my lungs deeply to match my breathing to the lake. Spread before me was nothing but water, like the ocean. It was so peaceful.

I dangled my legs over the edge of the pier with the water coming up just two feet below me. I tried to physically relax my body, hoping it could bring relaxation to my soul. As my heart began to calm, the lyrics from the song "Oceans" by Hillsong came to my mind. I started humming, which soon turned to singing. I am not one to typically sing in public, but this was not a typical moment.

I believed that as I called upon God's name, he would keep me steady through this storm. My soul was resting in God's embrace, and I felt a sense of peace and comfort rush through my body. I felt it deep in my core and spreading out through my veins. I knew this kind of supernatural feeling could only be from heaven.

My heavenly Father had heard my prayers, as aggressive and confrontational as they were, and met me at this moment to provide assurance and peace. In the midst of the pandemonium, I felt unwaveringly confident that God would see me through.

He was going to work all things for my good. I didn't know how or when, but I knew he would. I had no idea where he was going to lead me, but I was ready to follow.

I even felt a small spark of excitement for the upcoming year off of college. It was a blank canvas; I could do anything. The warm sun kissed my skin, it felt like I was wrapped in a warm blanket. I closed my eyes and stared up at the sun to take in the heat on my face. IT WILL ALL BE OKAY. I WILL NEVER LEAVE YOU NOR FORSAKE YOU, JUST AS I PROMISED.

The Lord spoke into the stillness of the moment and assured me with that familiar still small voice. Tears leaked out of my eyes, but this time they were tears of joy. I felt so safe and secure. Difficult hours, days, and weeks lay ahead of me, but I was confident God was going to see me through them. I could handle whatever came my way, one step at a time, because my loving Father in heaven was committed to taking every little step alongside me.

Lamentations 3:22b–23 says, "His compassions never fail. They are new every morning; great is your faithfulness." God's mercy and compassion are given freely from an unlimited supply. No matter my circumstances, however grim they may appear, his mercy is dependable and constant.

I answered God's voice out loud. "Okay, Father. I trust you, and I trust your plans for me even though I can't see them yet."

*** *** *** *** ***

This day was a distinct moment of God calling me out into deep waters where my own feet would fail me. I could not depend on myself and my own strength to get through this, I needed him and his strength. I chose to believe my faith would not only stand but would be deepened from this terrible situation.

I headed back to campus to prepare for a meeting I had that afternoon with the dean of students. We needed to discuss the logistics of my dismissal. Since it was the last week of class before finals week, I had actually already completed all of the assignments in a couple of my courses. I figured the school was forced to give me credit for those courses. Then, I figured, if I turned in everything in my other courses by the next morning maybe I could get credit for those, too.

I asked the dean about this, and his reply was "That is not something I have the power to decide myself; there are others involved in approving something like that. This is obviously a unique situation, and I see where you are coming from. It is very possible you will receive credit for the classes you have already finished, and maybe even for the others. If I were you, I would turn in everything you possibly can tomorrow morning and hope for the best."

I had informed my favorite professor, who I had two classes with that semester, of the case against me and the appeal process. I called to tell him the decision. In my Greek class, he decided to allow my grade to stand as it was, exempting me from my missing assignments. In my Romans class, he said I could take the final exam the following morning with a proctor in the room with me.

I was shocked by his kindness. I had not considered taking a final exam early as an option, since most professors did not allow it. This gave me hope that my hard work all semester might not be wasted. I planned to talk to two more of my professors the next morning to see if I could take their final exams early, too.

I stayed up all night completing my assignments and studying for my final. I became so tired the only way to keep working was to stand. In a nearly drunken state from sleep deprivation, I finally finished everything right in time for breakfast. I talked to those professors and both allowed me to take my final exams early. I took three exams in one day, two with *very* little time to prepare, and I aced all three of them.

※ ※ ※ ※ ※

My head slammed into my lumpy pillow when I finally made it to the end of that day. I breathed a huge sigh of relief and prayed everything I just did would not be in vain. Four days later my prayer was answered. My college agreed I was allowed to receive credit for all the courses in which I had completed all the work, which, thanks to my gracious professors, was all of them. My hard work had paid off.

My roommate, Sandy, was graduating, and right after her graduation we planned to start our final road trip together. So, even though I was done with all my classwork, I stayed in Chicago during finals week waiting for her graduation ceremony. Plus, I had many goodbyes to say to dear friends.

These goodbyes were particularly difficult because I didn't plan to return to finish my degree, but even if I did most of my friends would graduate in the meantime. Since I was banished from campus, I temporarily slept on the floor at a friend's apartment in the city. During the day I spent most of my time on campus, including spending a lot of time with Sandy.

One night we were talking about waterfalls, which we both loved. We had seen well over a dozen on our road trips. In our conversation we discovered neither of us had ever seen the largest waterfall in North America: Niagara Falls.

Graduating seniors do not have to take any finals, and I obviously was already done with mine. Thus, we had a few wide-open days on our hands. Turns out Niagara Falls was about nine hours away from campus. It seemed reasonable to us.

Staring at Google Maps I asked, "Are we really doing this?"

"Absolutely."

We were dripping with excitement as we planned out our impulsive road trip. I loved the spontaneity, I loved the massive waterfall, I loved getting to spend time with Sandy, but most importantly I loved getting away from campus to finally start processing what had happened. In our short trip I only scratched the surface, but at least it was a start.

After her graduation, we headed out on our final road trip together. We were bound for Tacoma, Washington, where Sandy would be living and working for the summer. We took our time through the Dakotas, Idaho, Montana, Washington, and even a little bit of British Columbia, Canada. This trip was full of the same ups and downs as the others.

However, our looming emotional goodbye helped smooth out most of the rough patches. In fact, it was some of our best times together. At the end of our journey, I boarded a plane to fly back home. We had exchanged goodbye presents the day before, and I still have mine to this day: a scrapbook filled with our wild adventures and road trips. This rocky friendship continued for another five months until it went down in flames over a 911 call.

Chapter 8: His Hands and Feet

You see right through the mess inside me and you call me out to
pull me in, you tell me I can start again. . . . I'm fully known and
loved by you. You won't let go no matter what I do.

—Tauren Wells

To fill my unexpected year off, I joined an interdenominational Christian training organization called Youth With A Mission. We abbreviate
the name to YWAM, pronounced "why-wam." YWAM focuses on training
young adults to participate in missions, specifically evangelism and mercy
ministry. I was excited for the opportunity to fill my time with something
meaningful.

I was accepted to join a six-month program called a Discipleship
Training School (DTS). A DTS is split into two halves, the first half is
called lecture phase. This phase focuses on training for being a missionary through lectures and hands-on learning experiences. Each week, a new
speaker or speakers came to teach on a specific topic. We discussed deeply
personal and difficult lessons through topics such as the Father heart of
God, the character and nature of God, healing from brokenness, hearing
the voice of God, servanthood, and the gifts of the Holy Spirit.

The second half is called outreach phase, and is spent directly applying
all we learned during lecture phase into real-life missions. My outreach was
in Southeast Asia. We focused on serving victims of sexual exploitation,
specifically those involved in sex trafficking.

My DTS was a heavy, serious, and profoundly powerful experience.
Yet even in this serious work we were doing and preparing to do, there
were wonderfully fun times filled with joy, too. I had no idea how badly I

needed this program in this exact season of my life. I was about to undergo transformation in a way I never had before and never have again.

※ ※ ※ ※ ※

I landed at the Los Angeles International Airport looking for someone knowing only her name. She was picking me and several others up to bring us back to the YWAM base. I waited around a carousel for my massive suitcase, which I had successfully gotten onto the plane despite being a couple pounds over the limit. That is one perk of being a young-looking, twenty-two-year-old woman. I stood at five foot four and wore my classic comfortable travel attire of sweatpants and a baggy hoodie, so I am sure, to some, I looked like a teenager.

"Hey there. Are you Adriana?" The cheery young YWAM leader had easily found me. I guess of all the people standing around that carousel I gave off the most "YWAMer" vibe. She led me to an area where other YWAM students had gathered to wait for more of our group to land. We had at least three more hours of waiting before they would load us on a bus and bring us to our base.

I am naturally friendly and talkative, but the excitement in the air brought out those qualities tenfold. I asked everyone where they were from, how they decided to join YWAM, what they were excited about, what they were nervous about, and on and on.

More YWAMers joined our group as their flights landed. One of them was Nora. Nora was several inches taller than me, with thick brown hair in a pixie cut which she constantly pushed over to her right side. She wore big round glasses, and had several tattoos on her arms, including a big flower on her right shoulder that I later found out she hated.

Despite a long trip from Miami to Los Angeles, she was in a chipper mood and joyfully joined in on our group chatter. I rattled through a cascade of questions for her. She seemed a little taken aback by my forwardness but happily obliged.

After an hour-long bus ride, we finally arrived at base. Nora sat next to me on that bus ride, and the more I talked to her the more I liked her. Sitting close to her caused me to notice her eyes. They were such a unique color—somewhere between the brightness of emerald green and the haziness of jade.

It was after midnight when we pulled in, so we quietly found our rooms and climbed into our beds so as not to wake up those who were sleeping. I nestled into my bottom bunk with a roommate I had never met sleeping soundly just three feet away.

My DTS consisted of nineteen students representing eight different countries. We were from different places, we were different ages, we had different opinions and upbringings, but we shared one faith: faith in Jesus as our Lord and Savior.

On top of having nearly identical schedules and having identical assignments, readings, and projects, we also lived in very close quarters. Seventeen of us were girls, and we shared one double-wide trailer home with two bathrooms. So, as you can imagine, we spent large amounts of time together every day. This proved to be incredibly bonding and we all became fast friends.

After only one week of being together, our leaders set up two testimony nights, but the logistics were far different from the testimony nights I had experienced in Israel. Everyone had only five minutes to share, but most of us shared for closer to ten minutes. These testimony nights brought about very deep, emotional intimacy in our group.

Since I was in a new place with new people, I felt the courage and freedom to share about my relationship history and my dismissal. I was still nervous, but I felt oddly confident that my story would be well-received by my newfound friends. Turns out I was right, and the escalated nature of our deepening friendships was amplified by these testimony nights.

Each one of us had vastly different life journeys, yet we had all chosen to leave our homes, jobs, schools, friends, families, and our lives as we knew them to pursue a unified mission: to know God and to make him known. These nights full of vulnerability further cemented our friendships. One by one we laid out our lives in their raw states. We loved one another an almost confusing amount for how little time we had known each other.

Looking back, I see this as an asset. A wonderful element of doing life together with like-minded believers. YWAM created an intensified environment for friendships to deepen and thrive in ways they do not normally. However, in my friendship with Nora, it was not an asset. It contributed to the development of feelings which went beyond the bounds of friendship.

We had only known each other for a couple weeks, but somehow it felt like a lifetime. This sentiment was shared among many of the new friendships forming in our DTS. Another way our escalated friendships manifested themselves was through physical affection. It was typical to find girls cuddling or laying on the couch in our living room, holding hands, kissing on cheeks or foreheads, rubbing or scratching each other's necks, backs, arms, or hands. All of these became part of normal interactions between me and Nora.

Additionally, we had ample opportunity to show our affections because we were roommates. We shared a small room with two sets of bunk beds and one other roommate. One night Nora and I were both up on the empty spare bed reading books. My back hurt from reclining against the wall so I moved to sit directly in front of her. She smiled and shifted to make room for me. I comfortably leaned back against her. Our nonverbal interactions became flirtatious, and I sporadically leaned back and angled myself in a way so I could softly kiss her cheek.

Looking back, I'm sure I was subconsciously testing the waters. Eventually, I sat up and turned to say good night, but I could tell something was bothering her. She wore her heart on her sleeve, making it difficult for her to hide how she felt.

I asked her about it but it took quite a bit of coaxing before she finally admitted, "It might be nothing, and I don't want to make it a big deal or anything . . . but I guess I don't know if I am just lonely or if I am actually falling for you."

She was intensely avoiding eye contact with me, and for a moment I was grateful, as an expression of shock spread across my face. *Whoa, I did not see this coming. I thought she was straight as a stick.*

I regained composure and we dove into the first of many conversations on establishing and maintaining physical boundaries.

* * * * *

Our attraction grew rapidly. Within a week, we had already broken our original boundaries and tried to establish new ones. Our struggle to maintain boundaries made our mutual attraction clear despite our efforts to keep from verbalizing it. Late one night, we were sleeping in the same bed, and in a moment of weakness I went from kissing her face to letting my lips hover just above hers.

It was late and we were the only ones awake. I whispered, "Nora, tell me to stop. Tell me this is wrong. Tell me you don't want me to kiss you." Part of me hoped she would do just that and the heat of the moment would pass. Instead, she said nothing. She couldn't say those things because, like me, she wanted this to happen. I sat up, feeling terrible for instigating.

I believed what we were doing was wrong, but I just could not seem to control myself. I wanted to kiss her, and now I knew she wanted me to kiss her, too. We sat close together in the dark stillness quietly discussing what was happening between us. We both clearly wanted to be more than friends, but we both believed it was wrong for us to be together.

The sinfulness of our love only intensified the already normal thrill that comes with a newly developing romantic relationship. Every touch, every wink, every line we crossed was thrilling, but the anticipation of crossing uncrossed lines was even more thrilling.

We sat with our faces close together and, just like that, it happened. We shared our first kiss. Part of me wishes I could say this was a beautifully romantic moment, and in some ways it was. But sadly, any romance was overshadowed by the imposing awareness that this was not only wrong, it was never going to last.

Therefore, as our secret relationship progressed, it was simultaneously enjoyable and upsetting. In fact, all aspects of our romantic relationship were caught in this paradox. It was both good and bad at the same time. I loved being with her, but I felt terrible for loving it. I knew I was failing to honor God, but I also knew I was starting to fall in love with Nora.

✻ ✻ ✻ ✻ ✻

The next day we stood on opposite ends of the room during worship. Heavy guilt filled my heart as I forced myself to sing the words on the screen. I tried to focus on praying about what had happened the night before, but my eyes kept wandering over to Nora.

Having traversed this road before I was more concerned about how she was doing than trying to deal with my own feelings. She had a wonderfully meaningful relationship with God, which was deepening further because of YWAM, and, above all else, I did not want to damage that relationship. But I knew, at a minimum, I was getting in the way.

Our actions were inevitably leading her into a place of pain and hardship. *God, please help Nora as she processes what happened. Help her to feel assured of your love for her and grace towards her.*

As worship wrapped up, we made eye contact, and with my eyes I spoke. "We need to talk." Her nod was all the reply I needed. We met up later that day and tried to hash out new boundaries. She shared a journal entry with me that she wrote that morning. I affirmed my view aligned with her own: sexual intimacy is exclusively designed for marriage between one man and one woman.

We knew the path we were on was one we could no longer continue. But the longings of our hearts overrode our convictions within days. We kept our romance a secret. We did not want to tell anyone, especially not any leaders. We were afraid they would separate us, or, worse yet, kick us out of the program and send one, or both, of us home. The secrecy led to isolation, and without any support or accountability, de-escalating our relationship proved to be nearly impossible.

One Sunday afternoon after church we had no plans. We went to our room to take a nap together, but no sleeping happened. At one point, she whispered, "I just cannot say no to you." I am sure she meant it to be flirtatious, but it felt like a dagger into my heart.

I sat up, clearly upset. She sat up next to me and wrapped one hand around my waist, and with the other she gently turned my face towards her own. "What's wrong, sweetheart?" My heart skipped a beat hearing her say that name. Sweetheart. Very few people have ever called me that. She knew how special it felt to me.

"I just . . ." I paused, deciding how to best verbalize my feelings. "Ugh, I just feel terrible about this whole thing. I feel like I'm the one instigating and like this whole thing is all my fault."

She immediately disputed my perspective, but I explained further, "I've been in this situation before, you haven't. And now I allowed it to repeat itself. How is it not my fault? Or at least more my fault than yours?" She opened her mouth to respond, but I didn't let her. "I knew there was a chance of me falling into a mess like this again. I should've come here with firmly established boundaries for myself, and I didn't. I let myself down and, in the process, I took you down with me. I am so, so sorry, Nora."

She aggressively protested my unwillingness to consider us both to blame. I reluctantly agreed we had mutual responsibility. I believed I was far more to blame, but she felt that was beside the point.

After a long, heavy, and emotional conversation about our relationship, and our clear inability to stick to boundaries, we reached a conclusion. Based on the notion that it takes twenty-one days to form a healthy habit, we believed we could break our "unhealthy habit" in twenty-one days. We decided to have zero physical contact for ten days followed by eleven days of hugging only. After the full twenty-one days passed, we planned to re-evaluate our boundaries.

In an effort to force ourselves to actually hold to these boundaries we agreed that if we broke them, we would tell a staff member what had been happening between us. Telling a staff member could result in a multitude of responses, none of which I wanted to experience. We felt confident in our ability to hold true this time, and the days began to slowly pass by. Ten days later, we prevailed over the first half of our commitment.

*****

I lay in my bed, wide awake. I rarely wake up before my alarm, but after a night of tossing and turning I was awake an hour early. It was the morning of day eleven, which meant I could finally hug Nora again. Finally I heard her moving to climb down off her top bunk. I sprang out of bed and buried myself into her arms as soon as her feet hit the floor.

Our six-inch height difference made it so I could perfectly nestle myself underneath her head. Our "hug" lasted over ten minutes, which doesn't count as just a hug anymore. We were clearly not over each other. However, this was not clear to us at all at the time. Our love had muddled our ability to discern concerning behavior and red flags.

Since our romance was still a secret, there were no unbiased friends to point out the obvious. So we continued on with eleven days of only allowing hugs, including hugs of socially inappropriate durations. We made it through all twenty-one days without breaking our boundaries, but now we only had one week left before flying out to Southeast Asia for our outreach phase.

During outreach we would share a larger room with more roommates. The pace and schedule were going to be dramatically different, meaning there was about to be very limited free time. This, we assumed, meant it would be extremely difficult to find time for just the two of us. In a very unhelpful fashion, this led us to conclude our final week together in the US was our final chance to be together intimately. We still talked about boundaries and wanting a healthy platonic friendship, but our romantic interest ultimately won the battle.

Part of me loved being with her and wanted more. We weren't hurting anyone else by our actions. But the other part of me felt terrible sadness and frustration for disobeying God. These two parts waged the familiar war in my heart. But familiarity did not breed comfort. In fact, the recurrence of this war only led to deeper anguish and hopelessness. During our last week in the US, I penned these words in my journal:

> I don't know what I want, I don't know my motivations, I don't know what to do, I don't really know much of anything. But I do know this hurts. It hurts in the long run and it hurts Nora. I am so ready for heaven. God, when will this end? Will it even ever end? How do I beat something that I don't even know I want to beat?

I felt responsible for my own pain and suffering and for how it was impacting others I cared for so deeply, yet I couldn't seem to stop. The last line was a question that had been weighing on my heart for years and I had finally put it into writing: "How do I beat something that I don't even know I want to beat?" That felt like the core of my predicament. It was a war in my soul, and neither side was willing to surrender.

I was a committed follower of Jesus Christ, and in the depths of my heart I wanted to honor and obey him. I had read the Bible from cover to cover, and I believed it clearly taught that God is not okay with same-sex romantic relationships. They are outside of his pure and holy design for romantic and sexual intimacy. So why couldn't I just surrender to *that* part of myself? To fully live in that belief and reject my sinful desires. Why? Because the other part was so deeply attracted to Nora.

I loved being with her, and I knew she felt the same way. I was well into the process of falling in love, and it felt wonderful. So why couldn't I just surrender to *that* part of myself? To call her my girlfriend and officially be together and live happily ever after. I couldn't surrender to either one because the other side of me existed. Simple as that. I was stuck.

I bounced back and forth knowing I couldn't have it both ways. I saw no way out of this war without full surrender. And I either didn't know how to surrender or didn't want to, or maybe both.

* * * * * *

Despite our secret romance, I still had a life-changing experience during lecture phase. Seriously, it changed my life. I was not just gaining knowledge about God—I was knowing him personally and in ways like never before. We had several speakers touch on the topic of that still small voice, a voice I had heard before.

I, however, did not believe I could ask to hear God's voice on demand. I did not think I could actually expect him to speak right then and there, when I wanted to hear from him. Turns out, I was wrong. Slowly but surely, over the course of about ten weeks, I grew in my confidence to hear his still small voice and have dialogues with the God of the universe.

Many, if not most, Western Christians have exclusively one-sided prayers. Sharing praises, thanksgivings, prayer requests, and intercessions to God. However, I believe prayer is designed to be a dialogue not a monologue.

One of the YWAM speakers, Pat Caven, taught us a technique for hearing the voice of God called listening journals. Simply put, these listening journals are structured as a letter written from me to God, and then a letter of his response back to me. In order to write his response back to me, I learned to carefully tune my heart, mind, and ears to hear his voice.

At first I found this very difficult. I struggled to determine if I was actually hearing God's still small voice or if I was putting my own words down on paper. I wondered if sometimes I just wrote words I wanted to hear. But Pat recommended no overthinking. She taught us, "Put pen to paper or fingers to keyboard and just begin writing. I can't even suggest what the first word could be, just trust that the Holy Spirit will prompt you. Just begin."[1]

Sometimes I heard only a few words in response, other times it was multiple paragraphs. Not everything I wrote down was from the Lord. But when I got done writing and I read over his response letter, I always instinctively knew the parts that were truly from him.

Pat's words rang in my head: "Not every sentence of God's response will strike you as significant. But I assure you, you will know that you know that God spoke directly to you. It may be just one sentence in two paragraphs, but it will be meaningful to you. On a number of occasions, God's response seemed to have nothing to do with what I wrote, yet it was exactly what my soul needed."

Over time and with much practice I grew tremendously in my confidence to distinguish God's voice from my own thoughts. Several months later, I wrote my listening journals freely and easily. This dramatically altered my relationship with God for the better. It felt as though I had unlocked a whole new level of depth and intimacy with him. I had chatted

---

1. Taken from a handout titled "Dialogue with God," created by Pat Caven.

with God like he was my best friend since I was eight years old, but now these chats were more tangibly two-sided.

* * * * * *

I knew my life was changing because as I called and talked with friends and family, many noticed changes in me, both personally and in my relationship with God. My mom was the most enthusiastic one to notice. She was extremely excited to see what would come from the rest of my time at YWAM.

However, another person who noticed was Sandy, and she felt quite the opposite. Part of the changes occurring allowed me to see the unhealthiness in our friendship and grow in my ability to establish and maintain boundaries.

I saw my friendship with her in a brand-new light. Over the summer she had, on multiple occasions, called and told me she was planning to end her life. This resulted in long and emotional phone calls trying to convince her that life was worth living. She was relying on me in ways I knew were unacceptable, and I felt trapped. She had successfully wrapped me around her finger.

A few weeks into my time at YWAM, I asked her not to talk to me about anything mental health-related. This was in both our best interest to combat our unhealthy codependency. I also made it clear that from now if she ever threatened to end her life, I would call 911.

One day, that commitment was put to the test.

I returned to my room after another classic game night with my friends. My phone showed four missed calls and one voicemail, all from Sandy. The voicemail was very intense. I called her back and defaulted to trying to convince her not to harm herself, but she hung up on me.

I called the National Suicide Prevention Lifeline. The woman on the other end handed me off to a supervisor who sternly instructed me, "You absolutely need to call the authorities right now. Every minute spent talking to us could be deadly. I am terminating this call so you can call the authorities."

Click.

I was shocked by the abrasiveness, but I complied, dialing the numbers with trembling hands: 9–1–1. I was calling from Los Angeles, but Sandy lived at a Bible camp in another state. The dispatcher informed me I needed to call a different number since it was a nonlocal emergency.

After re-explaining the situation to a new dispatcher, she told me a deputy was on his way to check on my friend. However, I needed to remain on the line. They did not want us contacting each other until they had eyes on her because they did not want the situation to change or escalate. I impatiently answered an onslaught of questions until the dispatcher finally got word Sandy was perfectly safe.

My call transferred to the deputy who had checked on her. He found her sitting in her room seemingly enjoying a regular evening. We had a very insightful conversation, I thanked him for helping my friend, and then I called her.

She was furious. "Why the hell did you call the police on me?!" She yelled and screamed at me for minutes on end without allowing me a single word.

Her language was colorful to say the least, so this is my censored summary: "Do you realize how embarrassing this is for me?! How much you just ruined my life? The camp director had to get involved, *and* my supervisors, *and* my roommates. The camp director probably thinks I'm a psycho now! And I'm sure everyone is going to ask me about this tomorrow, and what the hell am I supposed to say to them?!"

She hung up but called back immediately. She called me terrible names, told me to burn in hell, and said she wished she had never met me. I eventually got chances to speak, but she usually didn't like what I had to say and hung up. After hanging up for at least the seventh time, she called me back, and this time she was crying and apologizing.

As I sat in the little prayer chapel, late into the night, stuck on this roller-coaster phone call that I couldn't end, I actually felt at peace. I believed I had done what was right. I believed I was going to reap the benefits of my decision in the days and weeks to come.

Over an hour passed before I strongly addressed her. "Listen. I love you very much. I did what I did because I love you and care about you. I don't need you to agree with me about it, but that is the truth. It was out of love. But I'm exhausted, so I am hanging up now. I'm going to turn my phone off, pray, and go to bed. I will talk to you tomorrow. Good night."

I did call her the next day, but our friendship was never the same. She said I was different. Despite my best efforts to assure her the changes in me were positive, she remained unconvinced and we gradually grew apart.

I had done something out of the ordinary. I had established and firmly maintained boundaries, and she did not appreciate the ways these boundaries impacted the norms in our relationship. Which is understandable. Disrupting normal patterns is both hard to do and hard to accept, but in this case, it needed to be done. For the sake of us both.

* * * * *

Fortunately, the most important person to believe the changes in me were positive was me, and I was sure of it. I felt closer to God than I ever had before. I trusted him more, I listened for his voice more, and I was saturating myself in his word. Little did I know, more changes were in store for my life, my heart, and my relationship with my heavenly Father in the months ahead.

Outreach phase had arrived, at last.

I rolled up each piece of clothing as tight as possible so they would take up the least amount of space. Then I jammed and pushed all of my belongings down into my fifteen-liter hiking backpack as I desperately tried to make it all fit. Each person going on outreach was required to have one of these packs. Thirteen young adults with massive packs on our backs and regular backpacks on our fronts sure made us stand out in a crowd. Personally, I thought we looked pretty cool.

Armed with watches, water bottles, unflattering, modest clothes, and our Bibles, we made our way out of the airport in a disheveled state. Half of us were physically and mentally exhausted from the flights and travel, the other half were busting at the seams with excitement. I was definitely in the second group.

All thirteen of us, with all our backpacks, piled into our very first cramped ride in a *songthaew*. *Songthaews* are adapted pickup trucks with two rows of seats facing one another and a cage of sorts fitting over the entire back of the truck for riders to hold on. They are used as a shared taxi, and we quickly discovered that even when you think there couldn't possibly be room for one more passenger, they find a way. Sometimes involving riders standing off the back of the truck and hanging on for dear life.

We made it safely through that first ride and countless others as we spent four weeks doing full-time ministry in Thailand followed by eight more weeks in the Philippines. Our ministry experiences were very intense. We focused on working with victims of sexual exploitation. The opportunities to minister to this group of people were different in each of the countries, but nearly all of what we did was relational ministry.

That means our time was dedicated to building relationships with those we served, which takes a considerable amount of emotional energy. We put together a beauty parlor for the girls and women working at the bars, we conversed with monks at a Buddhist temple, we participated in a young adult's Bible study, and we led a Bible study for women living in the slums.

In Thailand, every other night we went out to bars to sit down for (nonalcoholic) drinks with the men, women, boys, and girls who worked there. These bars did more than just sell food and drinks. Worse yet, we knew some of the workers were there against their will, while others were manipulated and coerced into believing they had no other choice. Everything we did centered around becoming friends with those who were suffering. All of this caused our lives to be full of high highs and low lows. It was emotionally taxing.

Thankfully, our leaders did an excellent job of providing space and time for us to process our heavy and heart-wrenching experiences. We bonded as a group until we felt like one big family navigating this ministry adventure hand in hand. Some days were filled with joy and a sense of breakthrough, while others left us feeling both helpless and outraged. And while all this was happening, mine and Nora's secret relationship could be described in the same words: high highs, low lows, and emotionally taxing.

* * * * * *

Contrary to our expectations, we found a fair amount of opportunity to be alone together. Every little bit of free time we had, Nora and I wanted to spend exploring around the area. We always invited everyone to join us, but sometimes no one else wanted to come, so we explored on our own. Inevitably, many of these times together felt like dates.

One time, we shopped around a local market and then snuck into one of the tallest buildings in the city. We rode the elevator to the top floor, which was under construction. We were the only ones up there.

The full moon added a nice touch to the amazing view. I said a classic cheesy line of loving my view of her even more than the one of the city. Then I reached out my hand. "Excuse me, miss, may I have this dance?"

Her face lit up as I pulled her to me. We began to slowly sway to no music at all. I started softly singing "Dancing in the Moonlight." Eventually I forgot the right lyrics so I filled in with my own about us. After a while, I stood on a step so our height differential was reversed. We switched the placement of our hands accordingly. She leaned her head onto my shoulder and whispered softly, "I don't want this moment to end." I kissed her forehead and agreed, "Me neither."

We were doing our hearts no favors in allowing the fire of our love to not only continue but to grow. There was an unspoken assumption that at this point we might as well ride this out until the end of outreach phase. Then, when we said goodbye and were separately physically, it would also be a goodbye to our romantic relationship.

Around halfway through our outreach phase our two leaders did individual check-ins with all of us. Both Nora and I were asked about the nature of our relationship. My leader posed the question, "Do you think you have a codependent relationship with Nora?"

"No, I don't think we do. We really enjoy spending time together, but I don't think it is codependent," I answered honestly. However, I was also obviously omitting information which any reasonable person would consider to be on topic.

The "what if" moments in life can feel haunting at times, and, for me, this is one of those times. I will never know what could have happened had I been courageous enough to be honest with my leaders. Fear of the repercussions was certainly a major factor in my unwillingness to share. However, another factor was knowing, deep down, I didn't want help ending this relationship. Therefore, I remained stuck in this seemingly unending scenario which I simultaneously loved and hated.

Eventually our three months of outreach came to a close, and I had prearranged to remain in the Philippines for three additional months on my own. Therefore, as the rest of my team geared up for returning home, I was just reaching my halfway point. We were all exhausted from our intense ministry experiences, so our leaders booked a nearly weeklong stay at a very nice hotel in the capital city for a time of debrief and relaxation. Everyone cheered in excited anticipation for a major change of pace and a much-needed respite.

Nora and I joined in the excitement, but, under the surface, we both anxiously anticipated our impending goodbye. This truly felt like our last chance to be together, romantically speaking. The change of location led to new rooms and new roommates. Nora and I purposefully, and foolishly, opted for a room with just the two of us.

Throughout outreach phase we continued to sporadically steal brief moments of romance and intimacy, but now everything was coming to an end. She was leaving with the rest of the group to go back to the US while I stayed behind. It was a very real possibility we would never see each other again.

After our last night together came the moment we had been dreading. I had several emotional goodbyes to exchange, but hardest of all was with Nora. Many of our friends were within earshot as we said our goodbye which prevented us from saying what we really wanted to say. This was a predictable scenario, so we had both prepared letters as a feeble attempt to try to articulate our feelings. Then I stood outside the hotel and watched my team drive off towards the airport.

*** *** ***

I slumped down into the hard wooden seats at the local bus station. Large sweat stains had formed under my armpits from lugging around my heavy hiking backpack in the eighty-five-degree heat. I closed my eyes briefly and tried to process my emotions.

I felt excited about staying for three more months of ministry. I was sad about saying goodbye to my team. I knew for many of them, if not most, there was a strong chance we wouldn't see each other again. At least not on this side of heaven.

I didn't want to admit it, but I was also afraid of going from being surrounded by a loud and chaotic team of my close friends to living alone. On top of all this, I had the emotional turmoil of saying goodbye to Nora. We agreed it was wrong to be together romantically, yet we had fallen in love.

I believe there is a significant difference between loving someone romantically and being in love. You can make yourself love someone. It can happen quickly and with many different romantic relationships. Falling in love is rare. It is intense, and it takes time to develop. It is the deepest level of affection, and you can't make yourself fall in love—it just happens.

Nora's letter was burning a hole in my pocket, and I decided crying in a crowded bus station was as good of a place to cry as any.

She wrote a full letter, front and back. Tears welled up into my eyes after just the first few lines. Here is how it ended:

> How am I supposed to end a letter when I could go on for days about all the reasons I love you, why I am thankful for you, and all the ways this friendship has blessed me? I guess all I can say is that I love you so much, I am going to miss you like crazy, and that I will see you soon because I refuse to let this be goodbye.

I read it twice, then twice more during the bus ride. It made me smile, laugh, and cry each time I read it. After the three-hour bus ride, I stumbled out into the loud and busy bus terminal. I pushed my way out to the streets and squished into a jeepney, the Filipino version of a *songthaew*.[2] There was enough room for half of one of my butt cheeks to "sit down," and off we went. I held onto the bar above my head to keep from falling flat on my face.

I passed my fare payment forward and my change was passed back to me after multiple handoffs from my fellow passengers. After fifteen uncomfortable and hot minutes, I saw my host family's compound coming up and yelled up to the driver, "*Para, po!*" which means "Stop, please." I climbed out the back and took in the familiar sight and smells of my street. *This is my home now. Well, at least for three more months.*

I walked into my bedroom. It was the same room I had been in, but now all eight beds were empty except mine. A room that was normally full of clothes, shoes, toiletries, people, and noise was barren and silent. I turned on the "air con" and collapsed onto my bottom bunk, deeply appreciating the cool air. I looked up and discovered a large piece of cardboard tucked underneath the bed on top of mine. It was covered in sweet, encouraging notes and quotes from my team. Like a giant goodbye card from them all. Tears rushed to my eyes.

God had much to teach me in this season. Three months was going to be the longest amount of time I had ever lived alone. As an extraverted, high-energy, verbal processor, this proved to be a challenge. However, over time, I began to appreciate having my own space. Living alone also allowed me to grow in my relational intimacy with my heavenly Father who always kept me company.

Despite my sinful relationship with Nora and the battle raging in my heart because of it, I never doubted that God still loved and cared for me. In some sense, it is crazy I did not struggle with that, especially considering I was actively allowing something to harm my relationship with him. But the lack of struggle had nothing to do with me and everything to do with God

---

2. See page 83 for the definition of *songthaew*.

and his fierce pursuit of me: his beloved daughter. He never allowed me the chance to doubt him.

His love and commitment was abundantly clear in his word, the Bible, and in the ways he interacted and spoke to me. I knew he did not approve of my same-sex relationships, but, at the same time, I knew he promised to never leave me nor forsake me.[3] One rock-solid fact about God is that he keeps all of his promises. All of them.

※ ※ ※ ※ ※ ※

Nora and I now, by default, had a complete stop of all physical intimacy. However, the emotional intimacy continued. We kept in very close contact through messages and video chats. Some of our chats lasted for over three hours. Some were lighthearted and filled with flirtatious laughter and others were deep and meaningful heart-to-hearts.

She shared very exciting news of her decision to join full-time staff with a missionary organization. This was a huge decision for her, and I was so proud of her for taking that leap of faith. This meant she would be living in Los Angeles after my time in the Philippines came to an end, and part of the arrangement for my extended stay was to complete a debrief week in Los Angeles afterwards. Meaning I would get to see Nora again during my debrief week.

My three months of ministry was fantastic. One of my most fruitful roles was being a leader at a local youth group. I was the only female leader, so I also chose to start a girls-only Bible study to dive into some sensitive topics. This ignited a passion in my heart for working with teenagers—a passion I did not know I had.

As my time of ministry drew to a close, part of me just wanted to be back in Minnesota with my family, in my own home, and sleeping in my own bed. I had been gone for nine months. But another part of me was ecstatic for my debrief week in LA. Not only was I to be reunited with Nora but also two close friends from my team: Stitch and Jayden.

Stitch received her nickname while we were on a river in Thailand. We were horsing around on a couple of bamboo rafts when we both jumped into the river. I jumped feet first, but she dove in. After hitting a rock on the bottom, she got a considerably deep laceration on the top of her head.

3. Jeremiah 29:11.

Our bamboo raft captain stopped the bleeding with a temporary bandage of leaves and a headband.

Less than an hour later, in a wonderful display of her zest for life, Stitch joined a group of us to jump off a twenty-foot cliff into that same river. Eventually she went to the hospital and received five stitches. From that day forward I have called her Stitch.

So, in classic bittersweet fashion, I said my goodbyes to my host family and the dozens of people I had grown to love through my ministry opportunities. For the last time, I packed up that fifteen-liter, blue hiking backpack to the brim. I even managed to squeeze in a few souvenirs, including a wooden nativity scene complete with a palm tree.

After living in the Philippines for five months, I left it behind on a jet bound for Los Angeles. My debrief week in LA was an opportunity for me and Nora to prove we were capable of being friends without acting on our desire to be more than friends.

We knew it was not going to be easy, but we were determined to achieve a platonic relationship. It was the only way we could stay friends. But determination cannot only be in the mind, it has to also come from the heart.

Chapter 9: Friends with a Stranger

Oh, the overwhelming, never-ending, reckless love of God. Oh, it chases me down, fights 'til I'm found, leaves the ninety-nine.

—Cory Asbury

I watched the never-ending stream of suitcases and bags circling around and around the baggage claim carousel. My body filled with nervous anticipation. My phone rang; it was Nora. She told me she was waiting for me outside of door three. I spotted my bag and headed out the automatic sliding doors. I searched for Nora in the sea of cars and people as I breathed in the familiar smoggy air of LA.

The loud hustle and bustle of cars coming and going and travelers reuniting with loved ones only added to my nerves. Finally, I caught sight of her searching for me in the crowd and called out her name. Her head whipped around and her face broke into a giddy smile, making me feel like a million bucks. We hurried toward each other and smashed into a hug as big and wonderful as I had anticipated. I nestled in right under her chin. I loved hugging her.

We laughed and talked every second of our car ride back to our base. When we pulled into the parking lot, I could see Stitch and Jayden doing that cute little run where they already have their arms out for a hug and you aren't even there yet. I felt so loved by their enthusiasm and I was equally enthusiastic to be with them. As we embraced and exchanged happy greetings, I realized one of their friends was standing a little further back to make space for our special moment.

I had heard about her and she about me, thanks to our mutual friends. When she saw me notice her, she gave me a big hug like we, too, were old friends reuniting. Her name is Bailey.

She was also from Minnesota, one of our many commonalities. She had beautiful red curly hair that fell past her shoulders, sparkly sky blue eyes, and a cheery smile. I was a petite five foot four woman, but Bailey was even shorter and smaller than me.

Her style and aesthetic were deeply important to her. For example, she had a pair of white shoes that I loved to pretend to step on just to enjoy her aggressive reactions. She was a couple years younger than me and carried a youthful, sometimes immature, energy that outpaced even my own. She had a very deep relationship with God and was at YWAM to do an additional program after having already completed a Discipleship Training School at a different base.

In this program, School of Ministry Development, students read the entire Bible from cover to cover in only three months. Stitch and Jayden were doing it too, and I got to hear all about what they were learning and how it was impacting their lives and hearts. In turn they heard all about my time in the Philippines and how that had impacted me. It takes some solid and true friends to consistently dive into deep dialogues like we did over those five days together.

Nora was part of most of these dialogues as we tried to spend every moment together that we could. We never did anything inappropriate during those five days. However, our seemingly innocent acts of physical touch were communicating far more than what could be seen on the outside. Neither of us had moved on from being more than friends. The looks in our eyes, flirtatious interactions, and things we said made that abundantly clear.

Despite three months apart we were not even close to getting over each other. We never said it out loud. But we didn't need to, we knew. Part of me was deeply distraught, but the other part was excited to feel all those feelings with her again. Plus, it was flattering to know she also hadn't moved on from me either. *God, why does it have to be like this? Why can't we just be together?*

That still small voice came to my heart with a perfect combination of tenderness and firmness. MY DAUGHTER, YOU KNOW.

My mind immediately jumped to Adam and Eve, the first humans God created. They were the demonstration of God's design for marriage: one man, and one woman. And regardless of what I personally thought of that design, it was set by God himself. The one who created humanity and created marriage. Who was I to question whether or not it was the right design?

Admittedly, though, I found it particularly difficult not to question God's design. I wished so badly for it to be different, but it wasn't going to change. It was established and written in God's word and so I had to follow it. My whole life centered around following the teachings of the Bible—regardless of liking them, agreeing with them, or finding them difficult.

*****

Not being over each other was certainly a concern for both of us. After parting ways, we slowly started the process of determining what needed to be done. Following a couple of discussions on if we could be just friends, we took a full week to intentionally pray for God's guidance. At the end of that week, I was dreading our phone call. I could sense what was coming.

I went upstairs into the loft of my parent's home. Our loft was a big room, full of beds for when my whole family spends the night during Christmas. It was terribly hot up there in the summer, but it provided the most privacy. I knew no one would be able to hear me talking, or crying.

The tone of the conversation was somber and serious from the very start. "Sweetheart, I don't want to do this . . . But it has to be done." Her voice was heavy.

Our phone call was full of long pauses and tears. In the end it was decided we needed to cut off all communication with one another for the foreseeable future. I personally felt there were other options, but she did not. I likely just wanted to believe there were other options because the pain of losing her was too much—not because any of those options were actually realistic.

We felt this was the best way for us to move on from having allowed ourselves to fall in love. It was terrible, but we believed it was the right thing to do. Neither of us wanted to hang up, so we allowed the emotional goodbye to drag on and on until there was nothing left to say.

"Well, I guess this is goodbye then." I took in a shaky breath. "I love you, Nora."

After we hung up, I crumbled down onto the green shaggy carpet and wept. We believed it was possible God would communicate with us and allow us to become friends again at some point down the road, but for the time being this was the end. And now this brought about a whole new problem: I was going through the worst breakup of my life and not a single person on the planet knew it was happening.

This was a complete severing of our relationship, making it feel worse than a regular breakup. This heartache was so drastic and sudden. I was devastated. Secret romance had led me to a secret breakup. I was alone with no one to tell, no one to hold me, no one to comfort me. Isolation breeds isolation.

The secrecy that months prior had been thrilling was now suffocating me into painful silence. Thankfully, only ten days later I found myself with the perfect opportunity to share about our breakup to a girl I hardly knew: Bailey.

∗ ∗ ∗ ∗ ∗

Stitch was visiting Jayden in her hometown. Both Bailey and I wanted to go see them. So, despite the fact that Bailey and I weren't really friends, or were brand-new friends at best, we forged a plan to go on a short international road trip together.

She lived around the halfway point of my six-hour drive to Jayden's house. I beat her to our meet-up spot and sat on the back of my car enjoying the sunshine while I waited. There was an unusual dynamic at play between me and Bailey, and I knew we needed to talk about it during our long car ride.

A couple weeks before our breakup, Nora had begun confiding in Bailey about our relationship. She felt safe recounting nearly all of the details to her because Bailey was both a follower of Jesus and same-sex attracted. She was committed to a traditional understanding of God's design for sexual and romantic relationships, just like me and Nora.

I was grateful Nora had found a safe and trustworthy person to process with, but this led to our unusual dynamic. Everything Bailey knew about me came from Nora, and everything I knew about Bailey also came from Nora. Nora had asked us both for permission to share with the other, so we knew that we knew about each other, but we had never had a chance to talk about it, until now.

It takes a lot for me to feel awkward. Given my personality, I tend to not care what others think about me—which is a necessary component for awkwardness. However, ten minutes into that three-hour car ride, I felt very awkward. I stared at the road ahead as we caught up from the last time we saw each other. Externally, I was enjoying our various topics of conversation, but, internally, I was conflicted about how to bring up *the* conversation.

On one hand, I was dying to get this off my chest and finally share what I was going through with someone. But on the other hand, I didn't know Bailey very well, like at all. *Won't it be weird to share such deeply personal information with her?*

At the next natural pause in conversation, I boldly decided to address the elephant in the car.

"So, listen, I know you know all about my relationship with Nora. And I know a little bit about your story. And it's just weird that I know this stuff about you and you know this stuff about me, but we've never actually talked about any of it together."

She handled my blunt start to the dialogue with grace and kindness. She proceeded to walk me through her relationship history and expound on her theological thoughts about same-sex relationships. I was relieved she shared her story first. It created a sense of comfort and safety for me to share mine.

The phrase to "get something off my chest" really came to life as I finally disclosed the truth about falling in love with Nora. I sorrowfully admitted how much I was hurting from the breakup. I felt lighter just from having finally said it all out loud.

She continued to extend grace and kindness as she offered up words of validation and comfort. This allowed me to feel even more comfortable and share even more of what had happened and how we had allowed it all to happen. She didn't judge me or make me feel bad. In fact, she mostly just listened and asked thoughtful questions to keep me talking.

※ ※ ※ ※ ※

Our time in Canada with Stitch and Jayden was delightful. We ate poutine, mildly trespassed to go skinny dipping, went stargazing and storm watching, and, most importantly, enjoyed large amounts of quality time together. Bailey and I grew to be good friends over the course of our time in Canada, and afterwards we stayed in close contact.

Bailey knowing what I was going through created a deep bond between us. We often dialogued about Nora and how I was processing and recovering from the breakup. A few weeks after our Canadian adventure, I realized I needed someone to work with me at my small business for five days.

Bailey lived somewhat close to that particular job site. So, after sorting through some logistics and details, I asked her to work for me and received a text, "Okay, let's do this."

Working together provided ample opportunity for deep conversations. We talked through all of my past relationships, my dismissal, and my experiences at YWAM. I had never had a same-sex attracted friend with whom I could divulge my very personal thoughts and feelings. Because of her faith and sexuality, she could relate to me on a deeply personal level. It felt freeing to talk about my sexuality so openly. I had never felt able to do that before.

Yet again, I heeded no warnings from my past experiences of emotional and conversational intimacy. I should have known Bailey being the only person to know something as significant as this was unwise and unhealthy. How could I not know that, considering I had been in this situation twice before?

Well, whether by choice or ignorance, I somehow missed all the warning signs. I had a terrible tendency of not being concerned about the progression of a friendship towards a romantic relationship until it was too late. I misjudged the difference between a healthy, vulnerable friendship and a friendship that was heading in a romantic direction.

During those five days we spent the night at a friend's house, sharing one bed. At one point she established some physical boundaries. Given our sexual orientations this seemed both wise and reasonable. However, in my mind, the verbalization of a need for boundaries means there is some level of attraction. And like a child told not to eat a cookie from the cookie jar, I found myself tempted to do the wrong thing.

After we finished the job, Bailey came to my parents' house with me for a few days. We had some great times together sightseeing in my small community, swimming, waterskiing, and watching movies. But it was not all good. In this instance, I was right that the establishing of boundaries happened because there was attraction.

One night we lay awake, cuddling, with our faces close together. I partially initiated our first kiss, but after that Bailey took the reins. I sensed her desire to escalate the intensity of our intimacy, a desire I shared. That night and the following were our last two nights together, and escalating the intensity is precisely what we chose to do.

As with all the other times I allowed myself to enjoy sinful physical intimacy with a woman, I again experienced the antithetical feelings of excitement and shame. This time, though, the shame and guilt had an added layer: betraying Nora.

Bailey was not only Nora's friend she was also her accountability partner. She was specifically trying to help Nora manage her romantic feelings for me. And I knew I wasn't over my relationship with Nora yet, not even close. What Bailey and I did was messed up. I felt terrible about it, but I chose to suppress those feelings in the name of self-gratification.

After our two nights together, we parted ways. Five days later, I left for Chicago. I was going back to my Bible college to finish my degree.

✳ ✳ ✳ ✳ ✳ ✳

Despite the horrific experience with my dismissal, I decided to go back because I only had to complete one semester of classes and an internship in order to graduate. I came to peace with my unplanned year off and was ready to finish what I had started.

It is over an eight-hour drive from my house to my college. These hours were my chance to finally begin to process all that happened over the summer, specifically at the end with Bailey.

I'd slept with the girl who was my *only* confidant regarding my breakup with Nora. *Well, isn't that just great. And so on brand for you.*

I was in a new and complicated place of suffering. Being nearly an exclusive verbal processor, I timidly turned to the Lord for help. Questions came spewing out of my mouth with a harsh anger towards myself. An anger so severe it could rightly be called self-hatred.

"God, what am I doing? Why does this keep happening? Why can't I just get a grip on this? What is wrong with me?" Exasperated and furious, I smacked my hand on the steering wheel several times. I was yelling now. "Seriously! What the hell is wrong with me?! I am such an idiot!"

I am a firm believer that anger is always a secondary emotion, meaning it is fueled by a primary emotion. In this instance, my anger was fueled by sadness and regret. I was, in fact, deeply grieving my terrible decisions.

However, in the midst of my anger, I distinctly felt God's close and comforting presence. His presence did not bring condemnation or shame.

Instead, I felt his mercy and grace washing over me with reminders of how deeply loved and cherished I am by him.

This slowly melted away my anger. And all that remained was how I was truly feeling. It was overwhelming. My throat tightened as hot tears pushed their way to the edges of my coffee-colored eyes and started to fall. I reached into the glove box for a napkin to wipe my face.

God, why do you still love me after all I've done against you? How is that possible? How can you be so faithful to me when I am so faithless to you?

Sometimes God's still small voice speaks directly to me, but this time God brought to my mind a quote I had heard at YWAM. It is from Philip Yancey, one of the best-selling contemporary Christian authors: "There is nothing we can do to make God love us more. . . . There is nothing we can do to make God love us less."[1]

Now my tears flowed steadily, and I shook my head in disbelief at a love like this. A love which is truly unconditional, a love that is unwavering, a love that has nothing to do with my obedience and faithfulness and everything to do with his grace and kindness.

I drew in and exhaled shaky breaths. I needed to gain composure so I could drive safely at freeway speeds. I sat contentedly in God's presence for quite some time before starting to process again. This time I calmly worked my way through what had happened, and my involvement in escalating the romance.

ADRIANA, YOU NEED TO GUARD YOUR HEART. SURRENDER YOUR HEART COMPLETELY TO ME.

That was it. Guard my heart and surrender. I could do that, right?

I resolved to start this final semester completely surrendered to God and his will for my life, which I firmly believed did not include being in romantic relationships with women.

It was a fresh start: new classes, new friends, new roommate, new opportunities, and time for new choices. I did not have a new enemy though. He was the same and, unfortunately, he had located and exploited a serious weak point in me. The Bible says the enemy prowls around like a roaring lion looking for someone to devour.[2] However, I had a mighty defender.[3] I knew I could overcome my enemy, because he who is in me is greater than

---

1. Yancey, *What's So Amazing*, 70.

2. 1 Peter 5:8.

3. Deuteronomy 32:4.

he who is in the world.[4] In other words, the Holy Spirit is greater than the devil.

God promised to stand by my side and to help me.[5] But he could not force me to surrender. He cannot force anyone to surrender, that's the whole point of giving us free will.

I knew I played a crucial role in this spiritual battle. Was I going to stand strong in my faith and follow God's will, or give in to the desires and temptations the enemy threw my way? The choice was mine to make.

4. 1 John 4:4.
5. Isaiah 41:10.

Chapter 10: Facing My Giants

How deep the Father's love for us, how vast beyond all measure.
That he should give his only Son to make a wretch his treasure.

—Stuart Townend

I was twenty-two years old and incapable of gift wrapping a box. Plenty of people had attempted to teach me over the years, but nothing stuck. I could never figure out how to fold the sides, and no matter what I did the corners were always wrinkled.

My old roommate and dear friend Josie was getting married, and I was running late, as per usual. I desperately needed to find someone to wrap my gift for me but, to top it off, I didn't even have wrapping paper.

I frantically ran into our dorm floor lounge hoping to find help. Sitting there was a girl I hadn't met yet: Kyra.

"Hey, do you know how to wrap a box?" I asked in a panic.

"Yep, sure do!" she said cheerily as she got up to help me.

We went to her room where she found a newspaper to use and beautifully wrapped my present. I told her the present was for Josie's wedding, and I was so excited because it was my first time being a bridesmaid.

"Oh wow! Big day, big day!" Kyra enthusiastically replied in what I later learned was one of her classic catchphrases. I showered her with gratitude and told her I was embarrassed to lack this life skill. Then I ran off to catch up with the rest of the bridal party.

About a week later, she walked into the dorm floor kitchen while I was hanging out in there. We exchanged greetings and then I noted, "By the way, your butt looks really nice in those pants." I just meant it as an innocent comment, like in the way girls casually compliment each other.

"Oh, well, thank you. But just as a heads up, you should be careful with forward comments like that. They can be difficult for me because I am attracted to both men and women."

My eyebrows shot up and my cheeks flushed at her shockingly blunt response. I was partly confused why she felt the need to share that information with me in response to what I viewed as a relatively normal compliment, but I was also excited.

"Wait, really? Me too, actually!" My already loud and animated voice was even louder and more animated. I was so surprised to find a fellow same-sex attracted Christian at my Bible college. Plus, I had never had a Christian be that straightforward about their sexuality. She said it with a nonchalant ease as if she was telling me how many siblings she had or her favorite restaurant. She oozed with a confidence in her own skin that made me both envious and intrigued.

Now her eyebrows shot up to match my surprised look, and with a smile she casually replied, "Oh? Nice! Well, we should hang out sometime and swap testimonies then."

Swapping testimonies means to exchange life stories. While this may sound pretty serious, in our Christian college culture it was a normal thing to do. I eagerly agreed with her suggestion. This was an oddly brief and blunt conversation for being on *the* topic I needed to talk about the most— and who better to talk to than someone who personally understood my struggle?

As she turned to leave the kitchen, I was left in a whirlwind of emotions. I felt guilty for having carelessly paid her such a forward compliment. I felt ecstatic for the chance to connect with her about our testimonies. However, I also felt trepidatious because I knew I needed to be careful. I was finally being proactive in guarding my heart.

A few days later, Kyra and I sat in what my roommate and I affectionately called our "living room." In a tiny dorm room it is difficult to create hang-out space, especially when most furniture is not allowed. My roommate and I had lofted both of our beds and placed our desks underneath so we had just enough room for two little chairs by a bookshelf and a window. It was the perfect private setting for me and Kyra to swap our testimonies.

I don't think either of us anticipated the conversation to last as long as it did, but we just kept talking and talking. My deep level of trust in her did not correlate to the amount of time I had known her. However, it felt so easy to tell her about my past relationships. I was particularly relieved to finally share about everything that had happened with Bailey. It was still so fresh, so it felt good to confess.

I had only had about four interactions with Kyra prior to this testimony swap. We lived on the same dorm floor and attended the same college, but other than that we were essentially strangers. However, after we talked, it was clear we shared two significant commonalities: struggling with same-sex attraction and believing God's word teaches it is unacceptable to be in same-sex relationships.

Finding someone with these commonalities felt like finding a rare gem in a field of stones. A moment like that steps beyond excitement and into euphoria. Even though we had drastically different stories, she could understand me in ways others close to me who are not same-sex attracted could never understand. I felt instantly known and seen by her in a profoundly personal way.

In the safety of our similitude I asked her to be my accountability partner in regards to my relationship and feelings towards Bailey. She happily accepted the role.

* * * * * *

Six weeks into the semester, I had plans to head home for a friend's wedding. It is less fun to travel alone, so I invited Kyra to join me, and she accepted. A couple of weeks after we returned she invited me to her home in Michigan for fall break. Within the span of a couple months we had become each other's new best friend. But it turned out the cyclical and addictive nature of my sin was about to test my ability to bridle my fleshly desires.[1]

While spending time together in her hometown, our mutual attraction and feelings toward one another were becoming clear. We had been communicating our interest through nonverbal cues, flirting, and body language. Finally, we ended up sitting in her car in the driveway where we admitted our feelings out loud. We stayed in her car for over thirty minutes giving ourselves a pep talk and discussing boundaries.

Boundaries. I had an abysmal track record with boundaries. But I had stuck to them before, so I knew I could do it. I knew we could do it. We sternly expressed a mutual perspective of the sinfulness in us being anything more than friends and set our boundaries in place.

---

1. Romans 13:14.

Our boundaries allowed us to hold hands as we deemed this to be an acceptable act between friends. If other girls in platonic friendships held hands, why couldn't we? On our last night in Michigan we strolled along a river walk with our fingers interlaced. String lights and light posts warmly illuminated the path for us. It definitely felt like a date. She leaned in to kiss me more than once, and each time I pulled away. The last time I skipped away from her teasingly wagging my finger back and forth. "Mm-mm-mm. We can't be doing that."

Once back in the car, I more seriously reminded her, and myself, that this was not right and we had to control ourselves. That night, sitting on her bedroom floor, we wept together over the now complicated state of our friendship.

I woke her up very early the next morning since she needed to drive me to the airport. My flight back to Chicago was departing at 8:00 a.m., meaning we needed to be there by 6:00 a.m. I was whispering her name and gently rubbing her arm in an effort to wake her up slowly.

To my surprise, when she woke up and saw me, she grabbed my face and kissed me. I smiled from ear to ear, but found the strength to stand up and continue to pack my things instead of leaning in for more. This alone was a considerable accomplishment for me.

My display of self-control gave me faith that we could get past this and still be close friends. However, my faith was misplaced. I was trusting in myself—*my* self-control, *my* strength, and *my* determination—instead of trusting in God. I wanted desperately to prove to myself that *I* could resist the devil's schemes. But without total surrender to God and his will for my life, I was destined to fail.

Kyra returned to Chicago the next day, and that night I did not display the self-control I had previously. Since we were on campus, we found ourselves making out in the laundry room of all places. We hoped to not get caught, but also felt the rush of the possibility.

The following morning, I got a text with four words that made my stomach drop: "We need to talk."

She was extremely remorseful about what had happened and firmly declared it would under no circumstances ever happen again. Ironically, Bailey had purchased tickets to see a spoken word artist perform in Chicago and was arriving later that same day to stay with me for five days. The timing of the unhealthy progression in my relationship with Kyra mixed with Bailey coming to visit for five days felt like something out of a TV show.

The cherry on top was that the last time I had brought up "us" with Bailey she admitted she was still very much into me. So Bailey was coming, Kyra was anxious and jealous, and I had just made out with the one person who knew about my relationship with Bailey and was supposed to help hold me accountable. What an absolute clusterfuck.

I tried, without success, to assure Kyra that nothing was going to happen between me and Bailey. I promised to be completely honest with her. All I got in response was a sigh. She didn't even want to look me in my eyes, and I couldn't blame her.

The following evening, Bailey and I were hanging out in the lounge with a large group of my friends, including Kyra. Bailey knew nothing about what had happened with Kyra, so she was peacefully oblivious to the tension in the air. Slowly girls started to leave to do homework or head to bed until only the three of us remained.

My stomach was doing flips. If I had a device tracking my heart rate it would have thought I was out for a run. I desperately tried to act normal as I sat there with my former love interest, who wasn't over me yet, and my new love interest.

※ ※ ※ ※ ※

I lay in my small lofted bed that night, tucked in under my bright blue comforter. The unceasing sounds and lights of Chicago traffic came in through my closed window. Bailey was sound asleep on an air mattress below me, but I was wide awake. *Why do I keep jumping from one relationship to the next?*

I was caught in this awful cycle, and instead of looking for escape I just jumped on the nearest opportunity to repeat the cycle. I felt that familiar lump in my throat as tears pushed through my eyes and rolled down onto my pillow. An especially scathing element of my suffering was that, while I had these moments of pain and remorse, I knew deep down that I did not want to stop.

With Kyra it was even worse than normal. I didn't even want to try to stop. I felt defeated. *What's the point in even trying to stop if I know I am just going to screw it up anyway? That's all I've done so far, so why bother pretending like I am suddenly going to figure it out this time?*

I had set out to turn a new leaf. To fully surrender myself, my heart, and my desires to the Lord. And just over two months in, I had already failed. I have rarely experienced moments of self-hatred, but this was one of those moments.

I was causing my own pain and, subsequently, the pain of others. Worse yet, I wasn't strong enough to even try to stop anymore. I was giving up, and it felt terrible and wonderful all at the same time. I tossed and turned as I ruminated on my lack of desire to resist my sin.

Bailey and I got into arguments each day she was in town, so I felt a sense of relief when she left. That trip proved to be a clear end to any romantic interest we had for one another. We never stated that things were over between us, but by the end of that trip we both knew. It was an oddly seamless transition void of any heartache.

We stayed friends, for the most part. I am sure my lack of emotional reaction to our relationship ending was largely connected to the fact that I had already moved on to my next relationship.

My secret romance with Kyra lasted the rest of the fall semester. The amount of effort we put into resisting being with one another romantically varied each week, or each day, or each moment. Some weeks we instilled boundaries and followed them. Other weeks we didn't even bother pretending to resist, to the point that we went out on bona fide dates and kissed publicly. Something I had never done before.

There was a thrill to being nonchalant with our sin—escaping to the great big city, away from our Christian community, and pretending like our gay relationship was totally fine. It normalized what we were doing. Making it easier for me to try to convince myself that maybe being a gay Christian could be acceptable after all.

※ ※ ※ ※ ※ ※

During this relationship, I deliberately avoided personal interactions with God yet again. I was overcome with remorse and guilt the few times I did, so it was easier to avoid the whole thing. Though, surprisingly, I never missed a Sunday of attending church. At this point in life, I was confident my job prospect was going to be in a church setting, so I took the opportunity to experience a variety of churches all over Chicago.

Kyra didn't have an established home church, so she joined me on my church hopping journey. Each week we attended a different church, and I mentally or physically noted the ways each one operated. I then considered the positives and negatives from my observations.

Some weeks we flirted, held hands, and acted like a gay couple. Doing this in churches forced me to sit in my conflicted conviction. I was a follower of Jesus, a believer in the Bible, and a sinner saved by grace through faith.[2] Yet I was deliberately making decisions I knew displeased the God I loved.

Each week, sitting in a different pew or chair, I felt the weight of my disharmonious life. Each week, I heard a new pastor preach a new message from a new Bible passage, and, each week, I faced the same choice. Would I stop giving into the sin I was enjoying so much? Would I repent?

Repentance. Growing up in a Christian home I was familiar with this term. I was taught it meant to completely turn away from your sin. I had always pictured it like a physical 180-degree turn, and then walking away from the sin that was entangling you. However, I began to question if the foundation of my beliefs were rooted in Scripture or rooted in cultural or religious tradition.

Do my beliefs come from the Bible, or is this just what I've figured I am supposed to believe because other people in my life believe it? Specifically, my parents and my church family back home. Maybe repentance is just about remorse and regret, because I feel both of those.

In light of these thoughts, I turned to the dictionary hoping for guidance. First, I looked up *Merriam-Webster*'s definition, and it did not help my case at all. "Repent: to turn from sin and dedicate oneself to the amendment of one's life."

Displeased, I turned to *Oxford*'s dictionary, and this one made me feel a little better. "Repent: feel or express sincere regret or remorse about one's wrongdoing or sin." However, even this didn't bail me out like I had hoped due to one little word: sincere.

I could not say I *sincerely* felt remorse or regret. If I did, then I would also be turning away and amending my life. That is how regret works, right? People don't purposefully continue to do the things they regret doing.

A large part of me did feel sincere remorse and regret for my actions, but I could not escape the reality that some small part of me did not. And that small part was driving me to return again and again to my sin. I wanted to repent, but I refused to do so if I did not fully mean it. I felt trapped in

---

2. Ephesians 2:8

my sin. How could I escape when there was this part of me that did not want to escape?

God was gently but consistently knocking on the door of my heart, waiting for me to answer so he could speak to me. Mostly, I heard his caring voice calling my name. Beckoning me to sit and talk with him. Just two months prior I would've immediately obeyed, desperate to hear from him, but now I was resolutely suppressing his voice instead.

However, no matter how steady my suppression, his persistence was steadier. I was wonder-struck that, in the heat of my sinful rebellion, God was still pursuing me and was still committed to our relationship. If I dwelled on this for more than a couple minutes I would crumble in sorrow-filled acknowledgment of his grace and love. A love which I did nothing to deserve and did not deserve.

I could not emotionally handle processing an otherworldly love like this. In fact, to this day if I dwell on his faithfulness to me during that season of my life, tears will come to my eyes. His love truly astonishes me. And even though I thought what I was doing should outright remove his love for me, it had not even diminished it. Not in the slightest.

****

Just like all my gay relationships before, this one, too, was destined to end. It was as if that is part of what compelled us to ride it out and push the limits. We knew, in the end, a hard goodbye was coming, and then it would all be over. Which is exactly what happened. Except this one did not have a clean ending.

Fall semester ended with a week of final exams. Each student has different finals on different days, so some finish sooner than others. Kyra's only roommate finished earlier than us and went home—leaving us with access to a room to ourselves for our last night together.

The next morning, I forced myself out of her bed at 8:30 a.m. In a groggy haze I packed up the last of my things. We took one final load to my car which was in the parking garage. This was where we said our emotional goodbye. We knew this was the end of our relationship; it was unspoken and yet mutually understood. This couldn't continue.

I drove off to start my eight-hour journey back home. Like most of my long car rides, this one, too, was filled with tears and prayers.

We saw each other a month later. My flight for my internship departed out of Chicago. I returned to campus a few days before my flight so I could enjoy time with my friends, including Kyra. On the outside we acted like everything was normal, but inside we both knew we had only just begun the process of moving on from our relationship. Therefore, emotional goodbye number two came at the airport.

It was a late flight out on a school night so she was the only friend who came to see me off. We rode the blue line train to the final stop at Chicago O'Hare. Kyra had established boundaries before I came back to Chicago. Simply put, she allowed hugging only. As we sat stiffly on the long train ride, I broke the silence on the topic we had craftily avoided for four days: us.

"So . . . this might be the last time I ever see you?" I asked dejectedly.

She looked away and gave a little shrug. I could tell she was fighting back tears. In a discourteous and unhelpful move, I asked, "Are you sure I can't hold your hand right now?"

She answered my question with a look instead of with words. I gazed into her sad eyes and nodded to silently accept her answer: no.

She stayed by my side all the way until I had to enter the security line. A complete stranger approached us as we waited for my boarding pass to print. She happily exclaimed, "I just had to tell you two, you are an adorable couple."

We both blushed and said thank you. It was the easiest way to respond. Then this random lady disappeared as quickly as she had appeared, having no idea the impact of her seemingly small compliment. Apparently, despite following Kyra's strict boundaries, our nonverbal communication was enough to publicly give away that we were still into each other.

We sat down on a bench and exchanged a normal goodbye until I looked her in the eyes with too much passion and whispered, "I love you, Kyra."

This time, neither of us broke eye contact. She then admitted something to me I will never forget: "Adriana, you have showed me how I deserve to be treated in a relationship. And, as backwards as it might sound, through our relationship I now see what a godly relationship is supposed to look like."

I wrapped her up into a massive hug, and we parted ways.

✳✳ ✳✳ ✳✳ ✳✳

I am typically a chatty person on flights. I find in-flight conversations to be exciting. You never know who you might meet and what kind of stories they might share. However, on this particular flight, I was feeling despondent. I put my headphones in my ears and made my way to my window seat.

I shoved my backpack under the seat in front of me, took off my shoes, and settled in for the long flight over the pond. Inhale, exhale. I forced myself to focus on my breathing for a while just to get myself grounded. Maybe if I just breathed then I could get a grip on the emotions bubbling up inside me.

The past year of my life had been chaos. Three different relationships had ended within seven months. Nora in June, Bailey in October, and Kyra in December. And all of these relationships started and ended secretly, because they were with women. And nearly no one in my life, besides the women I had been with, even knew I was attracted to women.

I stared out my tiny window at the grounds crew working below. Kyra's words were ringing in my head. Surprisingly, what she said made perfect sense to me. Even though our relationship was wrong and could never work in the long run, God had still used it for good. He displayed to her how she deserved to be treated in a relationship built on respect, kindness, and faith.

God can take our poor decisions, our mistakes, and even our sin and use it to help us become better followers of him. It is amazing. Romans 8:28 says, "And we know that in all things God works for the good of those who love him, who have been called according to his purpose."

This verse brought peace to my troubled heart. God could use all my mistakes and my past relationships for my good and the good of others. That is how big and mighty of a God he is. He can turn *all* things around and create good from them.

However, this also brought to my mind the question that had been plaguing me. *How could something that feels so right and doesn't harm anyone be so wrong?*

I had struggled with this question for over four years, and I couldn't seem to come up with a satisfactory answer. Which directly correlated to my unwillingness to resist my desires. Some part of me thought maybe there really wasn't anything wrong with what I was doing.

Sins like stealing, cheating, lying, or gossiping all harmed another person. And sins like jealousy, pride, gluttony, or laziness were all harmful to one's self. But this sin, homosexuality, did not harm others and did not harm myself, so why was it wrong?

When facing this question, my mind consistently turned to the garden of Eden. In the beginning, God created humanity in a perfect world. In this perfect state, God created both marriage and sex, and he called them both good. However, he designed both to be shared between one man and one woman.

Yeah, well maybe the story of creation wasn't meant to be taken so literally. Plus, Genesis is ancient text from the Old Testament. It isn't as authoritative as Jesus' own words recorded in the New Testament.

But in Matthew chapter 19, Jesus Christ himself speaks on the topic of marriage by referencing the garden of Eden: "'Haven't you read,' he [Jesus] replied, 'that at the beginning the Creator "made them male and female," and said, "For this reason a man will leave his father and mother and be united to his wife, and the two will become one flesh?" So they are no longer two, but one flesh.'"[3]

It was God's design from the very beginning, and then thousands of years later Jesus vouched for and defended his design. I sighed heavily. I knew I could not get around that reality no matter how hard I tried. So while my sin was not harmful to myself or others, it was directly against God's intended design for romantic and sexual relationships.

I wished I could believe it was not a big deal. That I could say "love is love" and be with whoever I wanted. It is no one's business but my own anyway. But I couldn't. In my decision to be a follower of Jesus, all of my life had become his business. All of my decisions, my dreams, my words, my actions, everything was filtered through my faith and my longing to do what pleased God.

My entire life is built upon the question "Is this honoring to God?" I had chosen to live my life that way, but in this moment, it was horrifically difficult.

We were now thirty-six thousand feet in the air and the steady noise of the cabin, mixed with mostly sleeping travelers, provided a safe space for the turmoil in my heart to come spilling out. *Is my life honoring to God?* I knew the answer. I knew being with women was not what God wanted for my life, but I really did not like the answer. In fact, I grieved that that was the answer.

3. Matthew 19:4–6.

Chapter 11: Salve

Higher than the mountains that I face, stronger than the power of
the grave, constant through the trial and the change. One thing
remains. Your love never fails, it never gives up,
it never runs out on me.

—Jesus Culture

While the previous year had been a whirlwind, the previous month
had actually been one of the most healing seasons of my entire life.
I was home for Christmas break, and God prompted me to share about my
sexuality with two of my closest friends: Tank and Marisol.

At that point in my life, saying I was gay or bisexual was not an option.
I believed identity labels were inappropriate for Christians to use. I thought
it created too much acceptance of my sin. Instead, the phrase "I struggle
with same-sex attraction" felt more appropriate. This way I acknowledged
my feelings and attractions while also acknowledging my desire to not act
on them. It was a mouthful, but at the time it was the most helpful way to
share my experience with others.

I now believe labels can be used appropriately among Christians who
wish to identify as queer. It is a personal expression of a personal experience. I think each person should decide what suits them and how they pre-
fer to describe themselves. I also believe the use of labels can freely change
as a person's experience changes.

I'd never really had a "coming out" experience because it had never
been joyful for me to admit this part of my life. I took no pride in what I'd
done with my attractions. Talking about it with others was almost always
filled with fear and shame.

After sharing my story in a large group setting while studying abroad in Israel, I gained significantly more confidence. Since then, I had shared with many people, including group contexts, while at college. But I had never shared with anyone from home—friends or family—and that was about to change.

I sat crisscrossed on a comfy brown couch in the basement at Tank's mom's house. Tank was next to me, and Marisol was on the couch perpendicular to ours. I was completely resolved to tell them, but I was also terrified. They were both followers of Jesus, and I was afraid they would think differently of me, be disappointed in me, or be upset I had not told them sooner. Thankfully, none of these fears came true.

I took in a deep breath and opened with, "I have something important I want to tell you guys, and, in all honesty, I have been meaning to tell you guys about this for a long time now. I guess I've just been too scared."

Their tender, loving eyes looked back at me. The warm expressions on their faces gave me the courage to keep talking. I looked away and spoke my next sentences to the floor because I was too ashamed to maintain eye contact. I started off explaining how my relationship with Penny had developed in its unique fashion. I didn't pause long enough for either of them to interject because I wanted to get it all out.

"So that led to a struggle with same-sex attraction and I have acted on those attractions several times with several women." This had become my standard closing sentence. It made it clear this was a recurring pattern but that I wasn't going to walk through each one of those relationships.

They could tell how distraught I was to be sharing this. They were surprised, but they handled it with love and grace. They thanked me for being vulnerable and assured me they did not think differently of me.

Relief shot through my body like a drug in my veins. Their response was exactly what I needed to hear. They did not make me feel bad about my actions, they did not judge me for having done this while at a Bible college, and they did not turn the attention to themselves by saying I should've told them sooner. Maybe they thought it was weird, or gross, or shocking, but I couldn't tell because they made sure I felt validated, assured, and comforted. My fear dissipated, and in its place was a feeling of acceptance.

I recognize the word acceptance has unfortunately become its own hot-button topic: How can someone care for and support their queer loved one when they cannot accept what they are doing? Acceptance and approval are drastically different. Acceptance is to receive someone as adequate

or suitable, and to show them love, care, and support. Approval is to believe something is good or right. You do not need to approve of someone's
choices in order to accept them.

As an illustration, think of Christian parents who do not approve of
their son and his girlfriend having sex before marriage. Yet they still love
and care for their son and his girlfriend. Can that son still feel acceptance
from his parents despite their disapproval? If yes, then why is it any different to apply that same reasoning to same-sex couples?

Whether you agree or not, you can consider it food for thought. Either
way, I felt accepted by my friends that day in a way that was profoundly
healing for my aching heart. Smiling to myself on my car ride home, I
thanked God for such good friends. They had responded far better than I
had fearfully anticipated.

I WANT YOU TO TELL YOUR PARENTS NEXT.

I heard God's still small voice very clearly, but I wished I hadn't. "Uh-
uh, that will not go very well. I am absolutely not ready for that yet."

I WILL GIVE YOU WORDS TO SPEAK; TRUST ME.

I wish I could say I was obedient to God's promptings. The truth is
sometimes I am, sometimes I am not, and other times my obedience is
delayed. My anxiety and shame kept me from obeying this prompting for
five months.

* * * * * * *

The Holy Spirit prompted me yet again during that Christmas break.
YOU NEED TO TELL NORA ABOUT WHAT HAPPENED WITH BAILEY. This confession would feel like a double betrayal to Nora, and rightly so. Betrayed by
me for being with Bailey and betrayed by Bailey for being with me.

I was deeply concerned how this conversation would go, but I knew
without a doubt in my mind that God was asking me to do this. This time,
I obeyed.

Three months earlier, at the beginning of my fall semester, we had
become friends again. I felt a strong impression from the Lord telling me I
could reach out to her. The breakup had left us both with a glimmer of hope
we might be able to connect again someday, but I had never expected it to
be so soon.

Here is how we reconnected.

After God told me to reach out to her, he then said: BUT YOU HAVE TO BE PREPARED FOR ANY RESPONSE FROM HER. INCLUDING NO RESPONSE AT ALL, OR BEING TOLD SHE ISN'T READY TO TALK TO YOU YET.

I carefully crafted my text message.

> Dearest Nora,
> I hope this text finds you doing well. I've been praying and talking to the Lord and he's been talking back to me, so I wanted to ask you if you're able and willing to talk to me again? I'm sorry if this is totally blindsiding you and PLEASE take your time in responding. I want you to pray and make certain that whatever you answer is what God wants you to answer. I am going into this expecting you to take your time, so don't feel bad about leaving me hanging. If you have any hesitation then just say no. There won't be any hard feelings if you can't talk yet—I assure you of that. I love you and I will be praying for you.

To my pleasant surprise I received a message back that same day. Her response included: "I am very open to talking again! Which I assume you somewhat already knew based on the card I sent you, right?"

"Card?! I didn't know I got a card from you!" I had not checked my campus mail box in several days, and I was shocked to discover she had actually reached out to me first!

"I sent it like a week ago, sweetheart! You sure you didn't get it?" My heart leapt seeing that name again. I loved it when she called me that.

I jogged over to the campus post office and found her card waiting in my little box. I ripped it open right there on the spot. It was a lengthy card, but, in summary, she wrote, "You've been on my mind a lot lately, and I believe God is even giving me hope that our friendship will be restored in the not super distant future. I hope and pray he has spoken the same to you but, if not, I will still continue to trust in his timing. I miss you and I hope I see you soon."

Nothing could've wiped the big smile off my face. We had arrived at the same conclusion separately, and the Lord had orchestrated it so neither of us had influenced the other. We reached out through different methods, mere days apart, in accordance to his perfect timing. As I floated back to my dorm room, I praised the Lord for allowing this dear friend back into my life. I nearly happy cried.

After we got back in touch, we had a beautiful and platonic friendship. We texted and called an appropriate amount and for appropriate durations.

It was wonderful. But now, during this Christmas break full of healing and confession, God was asking me to boldly admit my sins to her. Despite knowing this could jeopardize our friendship, I surprisingly didn't argue with God.

I knew he was right. She deserved to know. I could not in good conscience continue to call her one of my best friends and purposefully omit a major detail of my life which directly connected to her. It was not fair or kind. However, also in the name of fairness and kindness, I reached out to Bailey to tell her I was going to tell Nora. She agreed it was the right thing to do but was glad I was the one doing it.

I scheduled the call and nervously rehearsed what to say and how to say it. When the day came, I felt as ready as I could be for this terrible conversation.

"Hey girl! How are you?" Nora sounded sweet and chipper as usual. She had no idea what was coming.

"Hey Nora! So good to hear your voice. I'm, um, well, I've been better . . ." My voice dripped with dejection.

"Oh? Why? What's wrong?"

I sighed. Then launched into it straight away. I was embarrassed as I stammered through a rendition of the events of that past summer. My stomach was in one massive knot, and I ended with a long apology. I knew we had betrayed her. She had confided in Bailey about us, and we had violated her trust.

The silence on the other end of the phone was deafening. I waited with dread. Finally, she responded, "I don't know what to say. I need some time to process before I respond."

Her voice carried a heavy sorrow mixed with a sharp anger. I apologized more. I could not say sorry enough for my part in allowing it to happen. I told her to take her time, and she tentatively planned to call me back within the next couple hours.

I retreated to the loft. The same spot I sat when we had broken up. The loft is unheated in the winter, and, being late December in Minnesota, it was freezing up there, but I needed the secluded space to pray and fret while I waited.

My waiting was cut short by a message: "Hey. I am not going to be ready to call you back today, I need more time to process."

Totally understandable. I felt terrible. But also, selfishly, I was unenthused at the prospect of having this conversation hanging over me like a gloomy cloud for an unknown amount of time.

⁎⁎ ⁎⁎ ⁎⁎ ⁎⁎

The next morning, my phone vibrated in my pocket. I quickly took it out and saw her name on my screen. "I am ready to talk. Does 1:00 p.m. your time work?"

I tucked myself away in a spare bedroom. When the Facetime call came through, I could feel the pounding of my heart throughout my whole body. I had never been more nervous in my life. I had no way of knowing how she would respond. But in perfect keeping with her wonderfully gracious character, she quickly quieted my fears and began to explain that while she was disappointed, she was also so sad for me.

Sympathy?! I don't deserve her sympathy.

A lump formed in my throat as she described how, in her time of processing, the Lord had softened her heart by allowing her to feel his love for me. "I just know God doesn't want you to be dealing with this anymore. He wants freedom for you, and he is grieved to see his daughter struggling." Her words stung with a meaningful conviction, but they were also a healing salve to my aching heart.

However, in the midst of this tenderness, she also spoke frankly and sharply about her anger towards me and Bailey. "I can't believe you guys did that. It is hard for me to wrap my head around, and I am still trying to come to terms with it." Frustration, disappointment, sadness, and tender kindness were scattered throughout our conversation.

Since this was going far better than I anticipated, I wondered if I should also tell her about Kyra. I felt convicted to tell her about Bailey, but since she didn't know Kyra, I wanted to leave that part out. I planned to tell her eventually, but it felt like too much at once. Plus, everything with Kyra was still so fresh.

"So how were things this past semester at college?" Her question shattered my inner dialogue. Given the context of our conversation, I knew she was specifically asking about my sexuality and whether or not I had gotten involved with anyone else. I closed my eyes and looked away in an involuntary physical response of how deeply ashamed I was of my answer. I dropped my phone on the bed, too embarrassed to let her see me like this. I held my head in my hands and sobbed.

Nora knew what my response meant without me having to admit it out loud. Out of a place of deep compassion, she cried with me. The woman I had betrayed shed tears on my behalf. Compassion that deep could only stem from her relationship with Jesus Christ, the Creator and Author of compassion. She was eighteen hundred miles away from me, but, in that moment, her love crossed that distance to meet me and sit with me and my broken heart.

"Adriana, I am so sorry. I'm so sorry you went through that." Hearing sympathy from the person who I felt had the most right to be infuriated with me was radically healing. I felt the love of my heavenly Father through my very special, and complicated, friendship with Nora. I felt I did not deserve her compassion and love. Therefore, I felt I didn't deserve God's either.

God had provided Nora with a supernatural dose of grace. He knew I needed to receive it from her in order to receive it from him, and his grace was deeper still. Unfathomably deeper. His love for me was not swayed by my actions, thoughts, or words. He is quick to forgive, abounding in unconditional love, and unwaveringly faithful.

This devastated me, in a good way. God was destroying the walls I had so carefully built to guard my heart from truly and wholly being his. He was tearing away all the lies I believed about myself and about him. He was wrecking my shame and shedding light on my dark isolation. In an impressive manner, he was bringing devastation to my chaos, my disorder, my darkness, and my helplessness. In their place he offered me peace, order, light, and help.

I cried for over five minutes without speaking. Nora stayed on the phone, mostly quiet, allowing me the space and time to grieve. She never asked for further details. She didn't pressure me to share names, how long we were together, what we had done, or any of it. I later told her how amazed I was that she didn't ask those type of questions and she simply replied, "I didn't need to know. And I still don't."

Our phone call eventually wrapped up and we hung up on very good terms. I shook my head in disbelief. *Thank you, God, for Nora. She is an amazing friend. I don't deserve her.*

I thought the prompting of the Holy Spirit to call Nora was for the sake of her knowing the truth. Little did I know, God had planned to use this to further reveal his love for me and help me heal.

God, I don't understand how you love me this way. It doesn't make any sense to me. My tears continued to flow, but now they were tears of joy. I sat on that bed basking in the immensity of his love.

Chapter 12: Vicious Cycles

When the world has seen the light, they will dance with joy like we're dancing now. I could sing of your love forever.

—Delirious? and Hillsong Worship

I popped some spearmint gum into my mouth to equalize the pressure in my ears. I chomped on it anxiously as I waited for my turn to get up, grab my carry on, and deboard the plane. Looking out the small oval window, I wondered what life was like in Nigeria. I had arranged to live here for five months in order to complete my final graduation requirement: an internship.

I had connected with a missionary family serving in Nigeria through one of my professors. Given my previous experience working with victims of sexual exploitation in Southeast Asia, this felt like a perfect fit. The type of ministry they were doing was very similar but in a drastically different context.

I had "met" this family on a video chat to do an informal interview. Now, after a lengthy process of securing a visa and getting properly vaccinated, I had completed the long journey and was eager to meet them in the flesh. I had a lot of cultural adjusting to do, but thankfully my host parents were more than ready to help me.

My time in Nigeria proved to be meaningful in many ways, including finding a friend to talk with about my story. Two variables made this friend unique to anyone I had confided in: he was a guy, and he was an atheist. His name is Sammy.

He was about my age, and stood a whole head taller than me with thick brown hair and a consistent smile on his face to match his goofy and fun-loving personality. My host family and his family were close friends, and Sammy was there to hang out and experience life in Nigeria.

He was staying in Nigeria for nearly an identical time frame as my five-month internship. After only knowing him for a week or so, we ended up sharing about our respective relationship histories. For some inexplicable reason, I did not even hesitate to tell him about mine.

He looked surprised, then his brow furrowed as he remembered our prior conversations. "Wait, this was at your Bible college? Isn't that, like, not allowed?"

I chuckled at the phrasing of his question. "Yeah, it's definitely not allowed. It was all in secret, and we were too scared to ever tell anyone from the school because we figured they would kick us out. Sorry if I didn't explain it well, but, to be clear, I also don't think it should be allowed. Like, this is something I struggle with and I've done, but I don't think it's right, and I definitely don't think God is okay with it. I mean, I know he isn't okay with it . . ." I paused because he looked like he really wanted to say something.

"Why do you think it's wrong? What's wrong about it?"

I knew he grew up in a Christian home, a conservative Christian home, so I figured he knew the basics. I got right down to it. "Well, I've read the Bible from cover to cover four times, and it seems obvious to me that God is not okay with gay relationships. And since I base my entire life around the Bible, then whatever it says basically settles the matter as far as I am concerned."

"But it's an ancient book written by humans. How do you know it's even all true? How do you know so confidently that it's even from God? What if some of the humans messed it up?" With this interjection, I jumped into the first of many deeply theological and faith-based conversations with a passionate atheist.

I appreciated the ways he challenged me and my perspective. I was forced to come face-to-face with why I believed what I believe. In explaining myself, I discovered it wasn't because of my upbringing, culture, tradition, or even my religion. I believed because God had revealed himself to me in ways I knew were real. I chose to believe the Bible is God's word.[1] I was drawn by God himself to build my life upon it. All of it. Even the parts I do not personally enjoy.

---

1. 2 Timothy 3:16–17.

Since Sammy and I enjoyed deep and personal conversations, we decided to go through a 2015 article from the *New York Times* called "The 36 Questions That Lead to Love."[2] To be clear, we had no intention of falling in love. We simply enjoyed the dialogues sparked by the thought-provoking questions.

While driving home from church on Easter Sunday we decided to go through some of the questions. We landed on number 33: "If you were to die this evening with no opportunity to communicate with anyone, what would you most regret not having told someone? Why haven't you told them yet?"

I did not have to ponder this question. I instantly shared my answer. "I would regret not telling my parents about my sexuality. And I haven't told them yet because I am nervous about how they will respond."

I stated these as simple facts, but immediately after verbalizing them, I felt sad. I stared out the window at the vast dry landscape, and I knew what I had to do. I needed to tell my parents.

As if Sammy could read my mind, he spoke out the exact words of encouragement I needed in that moment. "I think you should tell them. It will be good for you. Even if they don't respond in the way you hope, it will still be good to get it off your chest."

A week later was my birthday. Birthdays tend to make me reflective and introspective, and there was a lot to think about from the previous year of my life.

Here's the rapid-fire run down: One year ago, I was still serving the Lord in the Philippines; in June I saw Nora in California and then we broke up; in the summer I made mistakes with Bailey; in the fall I completed my final semester of college and got involved in a relationship with Kyra; Nora and I started talking again; I had a healing Christmas break, and now I had been serving the Lord in Nigeria for about four months. All in one year. I was hopeful year twenty-three was going to be better.

While on a birthday video chat with my parents, the opportunity to tell them presented itself as clear as day. My mom was an elder at our church and they were putting the final touches on a human sexuality document to clarify the church's stances. We discussed the document at length until I decided to walk right through the door the Lord had flung wide open for me.

2. Jones, "36 Questions."

"Actually, part of my perspective on this topic comes from the fact that it is something I can relate to and have experienced personally."

"Oh really? Wow. We didn't know that." My mom's voice didn't sound judgmental or upset at all.

"Yeah, it all started my freshman year at college. Honestly, it's kind of a complicated story about how it all started. But since then I've been involved in a couple different relationships with women over like the past four years." I was still terribly nervous despite a strong start to the conversation, and I was keeping things as vague as possible.

I did not have any interest in discussing names or details with my parents. That would be way too uncomfortable. Thankfully, my parents graciously allowed me to keep it vague. They asked a few follow-up questions before we seamlessly transitioned to another topic.

They never made me feel bad, they never made it about themselves, they never asked awkward or unnecessary questions. They just accepted me as I told them what I was comfortable sharing, and then we moved on.

We talked about it enough that it felt like a significant conversation without dwelling on it too long. They felt there was plenty of information about my sexuality that they just didn't need to know. We did exchange a more emotional than normal "I love you" at the end of the call. I think they really wanted to make sure I knew.

After hanging up, a rush of joy flooded me as I literally cheered and jumped around my room! I was so happy I nearly cried. What a relief.

* * * * * *

My time in Nigeria came to a close, marking the official completion of my bachelor's degree. I was still in Nigeria during graduation, but, all things considered, I no longer wanted the whole cap and gown fiasco anyway.

The day I graduated was logistically the same as every other day, minus the inclusion of one can of Smirnoff Ice. As a Bible college student, I was bound by an agreement which included abstaining from alcohol. So that one beverage was the only marked change of my accomplishment—a beverage I now find horribly sweet yet wonderfully sentimental.

I learned a lot from doing ministry in Nigeria. I enjoyed numerous cultural experiences I will never forget, and I met many amazing people. But it was time to pack my bags once again. I decided to treat myself to a graduation present of stopping in Scandinavia on my way home for a three-week vacation. Nora and my sister both arranged to join me as I visited friends from YWAM in Denmark, Sweden, and Norway.

International travel carries certain risks, including lost luggage. After landing in Copenhagen, I discovered my bag had never made it on my flight. My sister landed a few hours before me, and a couple of large sliding doors were all that separated us. We called each other to chat while we waited for them to figure out where my luggage ended up. Thankfully, two hours later, I was reunited with my luggage and subsequently with my sister!

Maybe it was because we love each other's company or maybe we were just overtired, but we had a great time laughing and catching up while we searched for our hostel. We got slightly lost in the process, but we didn't let that spoil our fun, and we finally arrived to the hostel at 2:45 a.m. local time. We had a jam-packed itinerary, courtesy of my inability to relax while on vacation, so we set our alarms for 7:45 a.m. No time for jet lag. We had places to go and people to see.

First stop: Sweden. We stayed a few days with a darling couple in their seventies who were friends from my time in Israel. They were the definition of perfect hosts. They fed us, brought us sightseeing, and happily explained cultural and historical facts of Sweden. Then we met up with my dear friend Sweedie. I am sure this nickname speaks for itself.

Sweedie picked us up at the bus station and brought us to her lovely little home tucked away on the outskirts of a quaint Swedish neighborhood. In stride with also being a perfect host, she invited us to sit at her table for the first of many *fikas* we shared together. A *fika* is a time to drink, eat, and enjoy each other's company. A delectable spread of jams and cheeses were set before us, along with approximately five different bread options. Swedes love bread.

In the midst of our adventures around Sweden I was determined to find time alone with my sister to tell her about my sexuality. I had been wanting to tell her for a long time, and I figured alone time would be scarce once Nora arrived. The opportunity presented itself several times, and I avoided it repeatedly. I was anxious, but I knew I couldn't perpetually dodge the topic.

My sister and I ventured off on our own one day when Sweedie had to work. We were strolling down a boardwalk on a beautiful sunny day, taking the scenic route to our next destination. I took in a deep breath of fresh Swedish air. *This is it, just do it.*

I cleared my throat and stammered through a rehearsed rendition of my story. She did not hide the shock on her face, but it seemed mixed with disgust. She asked, "Do you know of anyone else dealing with this kind of thing at your Bible college?"

Being so vulnerable made me more sensitive than usual. I interpreted her question to mean, "This kind of thing should never happen at a Bible college. How could you end up in a situation like that?"

I stifled the urge to be defensive and answered honestly. "Um, I really don't know. I only know of two other girls who struggled with this while they were there."

"Well, I am sure it is very rare to have a Bible college student messing around inappropriately with another girl," she curtly replied.

I left plenty unspoken while my thoughts swirled around my mind. *Why does it even matter? Whether it happens all the time or hardly ever, it doesn't change my story and my reality.*

She followed up with another unhelpful question. "Why did you wait so long to tell me about this?"

This question, by nature, made me feel bad. When someone is brave and vulnerable, they don't need help feeling bad for not being vulnerable sooner. I think my whole life would've panned out differently had I been vulnerable sooner, but I wasn't. So I, of all people, know I should've told my loved ones sooner.

"I don't know. I guess I was so nervous . . . and scared of how you might react," I answered, while looking down at the ground to avoid eye contact with her. *Scared you might react exactly like this . . . being disappointed that I didn't say something sooner.*

I don't remember what she said after that, but our uncomfortable conversation wrapped up. It could've gone better, but it could've gone worse. At the end of the day, I was thrilled to have it finally done and over with.

※ ※ ※ ※ ※ ※

A week into the trip, Nora arrived and she was set to leave four days before my sister and I flew home. Altogether, she was there for half the trip. She met up with us in Sweedie's hometown, Jönköping. A city I mispronounced the first twenty times I said it. We had been counting down the days to this moment for several months.

A thrill of excitement rocked my body when I woke up that morning. The day had finally arrived. Sweedie, my sister, and I all waited for her at the bus station. Neither my sister nor Sweedie knew how significant of an occasion this was for me and Nora. When I caught sight of her, with her adorable pixie cut and floral tattoos, I could hardly contain myself.

I yelled out her name and ran across the parking lot, even though this went against the calm Scandinavian culture. I slammed into her wide-open arms. It felt so good to see her face again. We kept our composure so she could properly greet Sweedie and meet my sister.

After three days full of adventure, good conversations, beautiful scenery, and great food we said goodbye to both Sweedie and Sweden. Our next stop was the capital of Norway: Oslo. My Norwegian friend Louise was attending college there.

She met us in her apartment entryway. She was dressed in ripped skinny jeans, her classic white sneakers, a cute flowy black top, and stylish sunglasses. Her outfit showed off her thin long legs and her good fashion sense. We spent our first day in Norway exploring all over the capital city. There was so much to see. We squeezed all we could into one day.

Louise then brought us to her hometown, and we stayed with her delightful parents. The next day we picked up our mutual friend Stitch. Stitch had taken a morning ferry ride over from Denmark, where she lived, and was waiting for us by the docks.

After enjoying Louise's childhood area of Norway, all five of us—Nora, Stitch, Louise, my sister, and me—headed to Louise's family cabin. We were set to spend a few days there enjoying the cabin's setting in a wooded area on the North Sea. Nora and I had now been together for nearly a week, and it had slowly become evident we *still* desired more than friendship.

Our affections had not lessened despite four months of no contact, eight months of being just friends, and even my relationship with Kyra. Quite the opposite, actually. My feelings for her were more intense than ever before. We did not verbalize any of this, but we didn't have to. We both could tell.

We knew there was a romantic passion stirring in our hearts. A passion which clearly could not be tamed by time apart nor having been with other partners. We had not fallen out of love. Not in the slightest.

Will I ever not be in love with her? Is it even possible to fall out of love once you've loved the way we have?

One of my college friends, who knew about the history between me and Nora, had warned me this trip was a bad idea, but I firmly believed we were over each other. I was genuinely surprised to find out I was wrong. All the flirting, long eye contact, winks, and provocative facial expressions reached a tipping point. A tipping point we seemed doomed to find. A tipping point we partially wanted to find.

It happened one night when we were the last ones to stay awake. We were setting ourselves up for failure, and we were doing it on purpose. Once we leaned in for that new first kiss, we threw caution to the wind. Like a stack of dominoes toppling over, one thing led to another, and we moved to one of the unused bedrooms in the cabin. Eventually we fell asleep wrapped in each other's arms.

In the middle of the night, we were startled awake by the sounds of someone moving around the cabin. We panicked. We scrambled out of bed, and, in a split-second decision, Nora hid behind the door and I crawled back into the bed to pretend to sleep.

The footsteps came closer and closer until my sister opened the door. She was looking for us because she was suspicious there was something going on between us. A horrified gasp escaped her lips when she checked behind the door.

We were caught. Red-handed.

Many tears and frustrated words were exchanged in the following early morning hours—mostly between me and my sister. She wanted to cut the trip short. "Either she needs to leave or we should leave. You guys should not be together at all anymore."

Thankfully, I convinced her that was not necessary. After confessing to Stitch and Louise about what had happened, we pressed forward as planned. However, my sister only agreed to this on the condition that Nora and I never be alone together and never touch. I obviously hated this condition, but it was far better than dismantling the whole trip. Plus, there were only three days left before Nora's flight home.

* * * * *

"Ooh, that would look so good in our apartment," Nora casually remarked while looking at a beautiful painting hanging on the wall of the art shop we were browsing.

A smile spread across my face as I gazed up into her soft green eyes. "Mm, so true." I approached the painting to examine the artist's abstract. "Oof, we definitely can't afford that price though."

"Yeah, we'd have better luck finding art at thrift stores and antique shops in Cali anyways," she replied with a twinkle in her eyes.

This was one of many forward comments we started making about our mutual desire and unrealistic dream to live together. Our, we, us. These words deeply impacted both of our hearts as we considered options of what a future together could look like. *Could we actually end up together long-term?*

After our one night together, the cat was out of the bag. I was wildly in love with Nora and I didn't know what to do. I had never felt this way about anyone before. I wanted to be with her forever. I wanted to marry her.

In wearing our hearts on our sleeves, we even dared to cover logistical topics as if we were engaged. Would we have a wedding? If so, what state should we get married in? Would it be outside, in a church, or some other venue? What would we each wear? Who would walk down the aisle? Who would attend our wedding?

In discussing this cascade of questions, we determined it made the most sense to either elope or move in together without getting married. A formal wedding felt out of the question because I was sure most of my family would not attend. My family would be confused, upset, and disappointed. And if most of my family wouldn't be at my wedding then it would spoil the happiness of such a special day.

However, our questions did not end with just wedding logistics. Where would we live? What kind of home would we live in? What about pets? What was our plan with our last names? Would we go to church together? If so, where? And what about our jobs?

This last question was a distressing obstacle. I had a job interview scheduled for the day I returned home. It was for the youth director position at my home church. However, even if I put aside that specific job prospect, I had built my entire life upon the goal of doing full-time ministry. I had talked about this since I was fifteen years old. I had poured four years of my life into a degree in evangelism and discipleship. Ministry is what I felt called to do.

If I chose to be with Nora then I was giving up my dream of doing ministry. My convictions of what the Bible teaches simply did not allow for me to do both. I considered the possibility of working for an affirming church or organization, but I disagree with their theology of sexuality and understanding of the authority of Scripture.

Affirming is the typical term used to denote a church or organization which publicly asserts that queer people are welcome in the full life and ministry of the congregation. Including membership, leadership, and employment. Therefore, these churches will perform same-sex marriages.

The irony is not lost on me that I, a same-sex attracted Christian actively considering marrying my secret lover, could say I disagree with affirming stances. Truthfully, though, I could not reconcile my desire to marry Nora with my desire to follow Jesus. I fully believed these two desires were in direct opposition. Therefore, if I chose to be with her then I couldn't do ministry. What would I do if I couldn't do ministry?

I could just work any nine-to-five kind of job. I bet I could find something fun to do. I'm sure I wouldn't love my job, but in exchange I get to go home to the woman I love. That sounds pretty nice actually. These types of thoughts enticed me to believe this whole dream was possible.

※ ※ ※ ※ ※

On Nora's final evening of the trip, we were sitting on an indoor porch swing in Stitch's parents' home. The swing hung from the ceiling and faced a big sliding glass door which led to a patio. My sister, being an early to bed and early to rise kind of gal, had made sure Stitch would "monitor" us so she could go to sleep. Stitch agreed and sat down to journal on the other side of the room with her back to us. When she heard us whispering, she kindly turned on some music to nonverbally grant us permission to have a private conversation. One we desperately needed.

I seized the opportunity to verbalize my inner turmoil regarding my job prospects and potential career shift. After she listened to my thoughts and fears, I asked, "What would you do about your job if we were together?"

Nora was still doing full-time ministry with an organization in California. She had been serving there for a year and was recently asked to join their leadership team. I knew she viewed this as a great honor. However, she answered my question without hesitation. "If it meant I got to be with you, then I'd quit tomorrow."

She spoke the words as a matter of fact. She didn't try to persuade me to feel the same way. She was just being honest. How badly she wanted to be with me made me want to be with her even more.

"Adriana, I *really* want this. I want you to move to California. We can get an apartment together. I'll leave my job and find something else. I'd happily punch a clock somewhere if it meant I got to come home to you. We'd go to the beach all the time, have so many adventures, travel, make new friends, and do life together." She stared off in the distance, smiling to herself as she imagined the life she had just described.

My heart raced and my cheeks flushed as I imagined it too. I smiled so big my cheeks started to ache. Brief comments and interactions had been exchanged, but this was our first full conversation since the night we slept together.

She whispered even quieter, as if releasing a secret from deep within, "Sweetheart, I'd do almost anything if it meant I got to call you mine." In that moment, there was no ring, no bent knee, no specific question, but it felt like she was proposing. Proposing the idea of being together for the rest of our lives.

We had talked about moving in together a couple times, and made many forward comments the past of couple days, but this felt real. To actually propose the idea of being in a committed, long-term relationship was something we had never said out loud. I thought my heart was going to beat right out of my chest.

Thankfully, she was not looking for an immediate answer. She had very clearly stated what she wanted, and now I could take as long as I needed to respond.

After a heavy but sweet silence she turned and looked at me with adoration in her eyes. If a heart could physically melt, then mine was a puddle. I loved her so much it hurt. I put my hand on her leg and she placed hers on top of mine.

In the tenderness of the moment I whispered, "I just wish this was okay. I just wish it was okay for us to be together."

She squeezed my hand, pursed her lips into a frown, furrowed her brow, and nodded. "Me too."

Those few words spoke on behalf of a thousand. Our eyes watered as we held eye contact. We had shared the sentiment before, many times, but this felt serious.

I wanted a world where being with her was accepted by all, including myself. I wanted my entire family to be okay with it and be excited about us being together. I wanted to tell everyone she was my fiancée, and I was in love with her, and not have it feel like a betrayal of my faith and identity. I wanted an extravagant wedding with Nora as my bride.

I wanted to shout my love for her from the rooftops without shame or guilt or embarrassment. Most of all, I wanted the God I worshiped to be pleased we were together. I wanted the impossible, and I wanted it so bad.

Chapter 13: A Crossroad

I couldn't run, couldn't run from his presence. I couldn't run,
couldn't run from his arms. Jesus, he loves me, he loves me,
he is for me.

—Chris Tomlin

Stitch's grandpa joyfully chatted with his granddaughter in the front seat of the car. I was grateful not only for his willingness to give Nora a ride to the train station, but that his presence prevented an awkwardly silent car ride. Nora and I were in the backseat, Stitch and her grandpa were up front chatting away in Danish.

Since my sister had no desire to say goodbye to Nora, she declined coming to see her off. This gave Nora and me the opportunity to hold hands the entire way, even though we weren't "allowed to." Stitch noticed but graciously did not protest. She knew this was a terribly difficult time for us.

Occasionally Nora and I exchanged long and intense looks which wordlessly communicated the turmoil in our hearts. We knew we were at a point in our relationship where a decision had to be made: either move in together or break up for good.

I had convinced myself that if we moved in together that didn't mean I had to openly admit she was my partner. I could call her my roommate to those I didn't want to be honest with, including my entire family. My sister knowing the truth threw a wrench in that plan, but I chose to ignore that for the time being.

Nora had made her stance clear. Now it was my turn to decide, but I needed more time. This was a life-altering decision and Nora told me to take my time.

CHAPTER 13: A CROSSROAD

The three of us—Stitch, me, and Nora—stood on the train platform with the large locomotive looming to our left. I took in a deep breath. We boarded the train to bring Nora to her seat and help load her bags into the overhead rack. Nora and I were aggressively avoiding saying goodbye so Stitch stepped forward to hug Nora. They exchanged a loving goodbye and then Stitch walked to the doorway to allow us some privacy.

I wanted to kiss her, but I felt it was disrespectful to Stitch. She was already graciously allowing us to break the boundaries my sister had forced on us and I didn't want to push it. I didn't want Stitch to have to feel bad for "allowing" us to touch.

We hugged for a socially inappropriate amount of time, but we didn't care. I nuzzled my face into her neck during our tight embrace and tried not to cry. We released the tightness but kept our arms wrapped around each other while we exchanged a goodbye. Our words felt empty. There just weren't words adequate to express how we felt.

"Here, this is for you." Reaching into her pocket she pulled out a folded piece of paper and placed it into my hand. I cleared my throat in an attempt to rid myself of the lump preventing me from speaking and gave her one more hug. "I love you, Nora." My hands found hers and I squeezed them both as I turned to walk away.

Stitch was waiting patiently for me out on the platform. I slumped into her arms, completely dejected. Thank God I had her there to support me. She could not possibly know how deeply I was hurting, but of all the people in my life she came the closest.

In a despondent state I stood staring up at Nora through the train window. It felt like a movie scene. I was in love with a woman, and I wasn't supposed to be. We were parting ways unsure if this was the last time we would ever lay eyes on one another.

Tears flowed down my face with soft sobs soon joining them. A man shouted in Danish, "*Alle ombord!*" And, just like that, her train rolled away. I watched until Nora and the train disappeared from my sight. Stitch touched my arm and gently whispered, "C'mon friend, let's go."

* * * * *

Stitch kept the conversation flowing with her grandpa on the car ride back. She occasionally turned to check on me or reached back to squeeze my leg. I tried to cry as quietly as possible so as not to arouse concerns or questions from her grandpa. Plus, the mass of emotions fighting to physically explode out of my body was unsettling. I definitely wanted to be alone when I unleashed them.

I fidgeted with Nora's note in my hands. I, too, had written a note for her. I hid it in her backpack the night before and hoped she would find it during her train ride. I should've waited for a private moment to read hers, even if it was just in the bathroom, but I couldn't bear it. I had to know what it said.

"Goodbyes have never been something we were good at. I just wish we didn't have so many. I have no idea how my heart got to this place or how I've been able to love you like this. It is stronger than I've ever felt. Regardless of the mess of this trip, I'm so thankful that I got to travel even more of the world with you. You are, hands down, my favorite adventure buddy. I pray one day we can do more of that. You are such a gift in my life. You are not the reason for our hearts being in this place, stop carrying that burden. I look forward to our next Facetime call. I love you."

My heart ached as I read her vulnerable words. I related to and agreed with every single sentence. I, too, had never felt a love stronger than this, and I, too, had no idea how my heart was able to love her like this. The end of her letter addressed one of my biggest burdens: I still felt responsible.

Nora was not romantically interested in women before me. I was the one with experience and I knew the pain that came with trying to be more than friends. Yet I had ventured down this road with her. Not once, but twice. I blamed myself for being careless enough to involve her in my cyclical sin pattern. The guilt I carried for causing her pain wrecked me.

I knew she was hurting, but I had to believe her pain was not entirely my fault. In reality, it was ultimately the enemy's fault. The father of all lies, the evil prince of this world,[1] the one setting out to destroy us and our faith. The devil is directly connected to all the pain and suffering in this world, including ours. I had to remind myself of that or I'd crumble under the weight of the shame I wrongfully carried.

***** ***** ***** ***** *****

I still had four wonderful days of vacation left, and I couldn't spend them sulking around brokenhearted. Stitch and her parents were wonderful hosts. Stitch showed me and my sister all around her part of Denmark.

---

1. John 12:31.

The fun adventures were a perfect distraction. I was able to completely enjoy myself despite a life-altering decision looming over my head.

In a stroke of coincidental timing, a friend of mine from Bible college came out as gay on Facebook. He and I had met through a student ministry group that did evangelism on the streets of Chicago. He was even this group's president for one year. I deeply respected him and his faith.

Part of his post read:

> For years I had struggled privately being gay and afraid. Afraid of God withdrawing his love and those around me believing I had lost my faith. I am not going to rant about the theologies or hermeneutics or even engage with personal opinions. Rather I want to inform you of this update in my life: I am in a happy relationship with my partner, Lucas. I also want to thank our amazing church; they have been such a great example of God's arms open wide to all. I just wanted to get this "coming out if you will" out of the way.

We were far from close friends, yet this rattled me to my core. To make matters even worse, his partner was a distant acquaintance of mine who had also attended my Bible college.

How could they arrive at the conclusion that God is okay with them being together? And not just the two of them, but they clearly have a church that supports their relationship as well! Is it possible that I am wrong about what I believe? Am I just so hung up on tradition? Or what my family believes? Or what I think I am supposed to believe? Maybe they're right and I've been wrong all along . . .

I knew there were denominations splitting over the topic of human sexuality. I knew there were churches marrying queer couples and hiring queer pastors. I knew there were thousands of Christ-followers who did not share my belief that marriage is exclusively designed for one man and one woman. I knew all of this, but this was the very first time I knew someone personally who was living out the life I wanted: being an openly queer Christian in a gay relationship.

The term "openly gay Christian" felt like an oxymoron to me. *How could a person be both when the two concepts directly contradict one another?* But now this personal example taunted my mind to wonder, *what if I can be both?* This man and his partner had studied the Bible at the same school as me. He had passionate faith in Jesus, which I had witnessed with my own eyes.

Yet somehow, someway, he firmly believed God and the Bible were not opposed to his gay relationship. I knew he and his boyfriend represented hundreds, maybe thousands, of other same-sex Christian couples who believe the Bible does not condemn gay relationships. All of this left me rattled.

*** *** ***

After a five-hour bus ride to Copenhagen, a ten-hour flight to Chicago, and a nine-hour overnight bus ride to Minneapolis, I was finally back home. Choosing to believe I am immune to jet lag and travel fatigue, I had scheduled my job interview for that same evening. A group of people in leadership from my home church gathered to conduct my interview.

It felt like a formality. I had grown up in that church since I was four, and nearly every person conducting the interview had known me for most of my life. They knew almost everything on my résumé already since they had heard all about my college experiences and my international ministry opportunities. Plus, they told me I was the only one who had applied for the job.

When the topic of a major weeklong youth conference came up, I informed them I would plan to attend if they hired me. They were happily surprised to hear my willingness to attend considering it was such short notice. The event was only a month away. This upcoming youth event expedited the hiring process even more because there was paperwork to be filled out as soon as possible.

They asked me to come in the following morning to sign some paperwork and meet with the interim pastor. I was under the impression the elders of the church had to give the final stamp of approval in my hiring process, so I viewed this meeting as a secondary interview. To my surprise, the interim pastor began discussing salary, benefits, paid time off, and the like. Eventually, I interjected to express my confusion.

"Oh, the elders received the recommendation from the youth commission by email yesterday and they decided a physical meeting was unnecessary and took a vote by email. The job is yours if you want it."

His words caused an enormous spark of excitement inside my heart. That's it, I was hired. I eagerly accepted the position.

"Great. How soon can you start?"

I pondered briefly. "Well, I can start as soon as tomorrow morning, actually." We shook hands and I made plans to move in to my office the next morning.

The prospect of flying off to California to be with Nora was still in the back of my mind, and now I was in a serious time crunch to make up my mind. I didn't want to start this job only to abandon it. That would be rude. So I had twenty-four hours to officially make up my mind. Talk about pressure.

※ ※ ※ ※ ※ ※

A noteworthy factor in my decision making was the stance of my home church on human sexuality. They hold a traditional stance, meaning they believe romantic relationships are designed to be between one man and one woman and sex is exclusively designed for marriage.

This stance is also held by my Bible college, YWAM, and nearly all of my family. And, up until my tumultuous and heartbreaking goodbye to Nora, I would've said I firmly believed in a traditional stance, too. But now, for the first time in my life, I genuinely doubted whether or not the Bible taught that being in a gay relationship was wrong.

With those doubts swirling in my mind, I decided to reach out to my dear friend and accountability partner, Avery. She was the first person I ever told I was in a gay relationship, even though I didn't use those words at the time, and it went poorly. Our friendship changed after that moment, and I wasn't sure we would remain friends at all. But a year later, out of the blue, she sent me this message.

> Hey, when you were vulnerable with me last spring break, I did not respond out of love. I didn't know what to do, and now I mourn the way I treated you. I wish I could've been there for you in the way Christ would've been. I want you to know I am sorry for the damage I have created and I apologize for any hurts that are still present because of it. I am sorry if I at any point damaged your self-worth and I just felt that I needed to share that.

I deeply respected the humility and care displayed by her apology, and I assured her of my forgiveness. She had gained a new perspective and boldly addressed her mistake of not responding well. She did this one year later, but even if it had been four years later or forty years later, I know it would've meant a lot to me.

Also, even if I had not responded well to her apology, she still did the right thing simply because it was the right thing to do.[2] I am a firm believer that it is never too late to say you are sorry. Avery not only sent the apology text, but she followed up with me about it the next time she saw me. I felt deeply loved because of her initiative and desire to make amends.

We confided in one another greatly over the following four years, and cultivated a close friendship. I told her about my relationships with Sandy, Nora, and Bailey. And while developing feelings for Kyra, I asked her to hold me accountable. In turn, she confided in me about her own struggles with same-sex attraction.

I was surprised by the irony, but was so grateful she trusted me enough to tell me. We had countless deep heart-to-hearts and wrestled through the battle of honoring God with our sexuality and relationships. Therefore, she was the perfect person to confide in about the crossroads moment I was facing. I knew I needed to call her.

✳✳ ✳✳ ✳✳ ✳✳

Do I accept this job and decide to believe in a traditional stance on human sexuality? Or do I buy a plane ticket to California to be with the woman I love?

My heart was conflicted. I wanted both, but I knew I could not have both. On the phone Avery spoke strongly, and even harshly. "You have to be honest with those in leadership at your church. Start with the interim pastor at least. Tell him the truth of what happened in Scandinavia and that you are wrestling with your beliefs in this matter."

"Well, if I tell him I'm wrestling then he will say I can't have the job unless I can agree to the church's stances. I signed a document yesterday that was specifically stating my agreement to their stance on human sexuality. So I know I can't stay there if I truly don't know what I believe." Since I am a verbal processor, the weight of my situation dawned on me as my ears heard the words out of my own mouth. What a mess.

"Then you have to decide what you believe." She spoke very matter-of-factly.

"Tonight?!"

"Well, before you go talk to the pastor."

---

2. Luke 17:4.

"But even if I decide I agree with the church's stance on human sexuality and tell him everything, then he will probably want to tell the elders. And my mom is an elder. What if he wants me to be the one to tell them? What if they ask me specific questions? Like awkward questions? And what if I do all this only for them to decide this is too concerning for me to have the job after all." My fears spilled out of my mouth, one after another like water out of a firehose.

"Avery, I don't know if I can do this."

"You can do it. I know you can. It is the right thing to do. Take some time to really think and pray, and I am confident God will prompt you to do the right thing. But I do really believe you need to be honest with your leadership. That is the only way your job will start off on the right foot. It has to start from a place of honesty and transparency. You can't hide secrets like this. It just isn't fair to them, or to yourself." Her words were clear and straight to the point. I knew she was right.

She continued, "Also, I think deep down in your heart you already know what you believe about human sexuality. I think if you actually didn't know then you wouldn't have accepted the job and signed that document in the first place."

A long pause followed allowing me space to sit with those words. I didn't know what to say.

She broke the silence. "Either way, at this point you need to talk to your heavenly Father far more than you need to talk to me. I think you know the right thing to do, and I believe you will do it. Think of it like a daughter going to her dad's throne room just to ask some questions and process with him." With that Avery lovingly wrapped up our phone call as I begrudgingly agreed to do what she suggested.

I prayed earnestly. I wept. I yelled. I cussed. And I wept some more.

After all that, I sadly did not arrive at any conclusion. It was very late at night, or more accurately early in the morning, and my eyes were heavy and sore. My bed was calling my name, so I chose to revisit this in the morning.

***** *****

Plagued by racing thoughts that night, I woke up feeling like I had only taken a fifteen-minute nap. I filled my lungs and exhaled slowly. Today was a big day. I got ready like any other morning. My parents and sister were all home, but they knew nothing of my inner turmoil. In fact, Avery was the only person who knew.

Since they didn't know, I packed up a large quantity of items into my beat-up Mercury Sable. I needed to maintain the appearance that I was moving into my office. I was in no way trying to be deceptive. I just knew I needed to make this decision on my own, and involving other people with their thoughts and opinions was too exhausting and time consuming.

I pulled into the church parking lot. *God, please help me. I have to decide.*

I checked in with the interim pastor and told him I had some personal things to sort through. We made tentative plans to meet in the early afternoon to finish up some logistics and paperwork. He was in a pleasant mood and kindly agreed to my unusual "first day" at work. With that settled, I closed and locked the door to "my" office.

A large wooden desk, a chair, a couch, scattered youth pastor curriculum books on a shelf, and a couple of posters left hung up on the walls were the only things in the room. I had carried inside my laptop, a notebook, and my Bible. I was resolved to sit in there for as long as it took to make a decision.

I opened my laptop to a blank page. It had been a long time since I had completed a listening journal. Far too long. I desperately needed to hear God's voice. In fact, I was more desperate than ever before in my life.

Thankfully, God knows all things.[3] He knew how badly I needed him and spoke to me in a profound way. Historically, my listening journals maintained a basic structure. I wrote a letter to God, then I listened for his still small voice to prompt me to write a letter back to myself. However, this time that basic structure was thrown out the window. This time, sitting in an office that could be mine, it was different.

I had an entire dialogue with God in writing. Back and forth we spoke, as if he was sitting right there in the room with me. I was reminded of the times I spent sitting with God up in the big oak tree at my grandpa's cabin. I didn't hear God's voice back then in the same way I had learned to hear it now, but my heart's yearning to be with him was the same.

As a little girl I loved sitting in his presence, I was carefree and life was practically void of decision-making. Now, as an adult, facing a monumental decision, I desperately needed his presence. But in both times in my life, my feelings towards God were the same: he was my good Father who loved

3. 1 John 3:20.

me and I loved him. Simple as that. I attempted to remind myself of those simple truths, but in the midst of my complex situation it was difficult.

※ ※ ※ ※ ※

Per Avery's suggestion, I thought of my conversation with God like a daughter talking to her dad. I came before the God of the universe in my broken state and poured out my heart.

"I feel so lost, so confused, so hurt, and so broken. I have felt similar to this before, but this is different. This time I allowed part of my heart to open to the idea that this sin might actually be okay. I have brothers and sisters in my spiritual family who believe that. And I just don't get it. I don't understand how we come to such different interpretations of the same text. Maybe we have just been misreading the text for so long. Could that be, Abba? Could it be that being gay is acceptable to you?"

I didn't want to use Google to find my answer, nor listen to the perspectives of other people such as authors, pastors, professors, or theologians. I wanted to hear from God. If everyone else in the whole Christian faith approved of gay relationships but God told me he did not approve, then I would stand on that alone. So I started in the most logical place when seeking the voice of God: the Bible.

I wrote out the primary seven Bible passages that mention homosexuality. I had looked up these passages so many times that I knew them by heart. However, this time I was reading them through a different lens than normal. I usually read them with utmost respect for the authority of God's word and conceded to them easily. Not this time.

This time I was looking them up with a singular mission: prove they did not apply to my monogamous, loving relationship with Nora. If I could prove this to myself, then we could be together. I was willing to bend and twist the words of the Bible to conform to what I wanted.

Four of the seven passages come from the Old Testament, and I stubbornly rejected all of them. I told God it was too confusing to navigate which parts of the Old Testament remained the same and which shifted under the new covenant. The new covenant was established by Jesus Christ and in Matthew 5:17 Jesus said, "Do not think that I have come to abolish the Law or the Prophets; I have not come to abolish them but to fulfill them."

Fulfilling the Law means Jesus completed all the promises and prophecies outlined in the Old Testament. His coming allows us to further understand the laws in the Old Testament. For example, in Matthew 5:38–39 Jesus explains, "You have heard that it was said, 'Eye for eye, and tooth for tooth' [Exodus 21:24]. But I tell you, do not resist an evil person. If anyone slaps you on the right cheek, turn to them the other cheek also."

Jesus fulfilled this law of seeking for all things to be righted in a very literal way, eye for eye and tooth for tooth, and instead commands us to not seek retribution in this way. Jesus explains how we are now to turn the other cheek and offer forgiveness and grace. What changed? Jesus came. His very life was a radical display of forgiveness and grace, and from that well outpours our own.

So how was I supposed to know what I had to follow anymore? For example, the Old Testament forbids eating meat with the blood still in it, cutting the hair on the sides of your head, and wearing clothes woven of two kinds of material.[4] Yet nearly every Bible-believing Christian today agrees those three things are permissible. What changed? Jesus fulfilled the law.

The Old Testament also forbids worshiping other gods, stealing, murdering, and committing adultery.[5] Yet nearly every Bible-believing Christian today agrees those four things are not permissible. Why didn't our following of those laws change with Jesus' fulfilling of the law?

How am I supposed to know which laws apply to me? We are bound by some and not others. It's too confusing. And what if all four of the Old Testament passages on homosexuality aren't applicable to us anymore? At least not in the same way they were then? Maybe I am just wasting my time reading them in the first place.

Though I grappled with these thoughts, in all honesty, I confidently knew which laws still apply to us today. I was familiar with differentiating between ceremonial laws, civil laws, and moral laws, and how they were fulfilled by Jesus.

My unfounded claim of confusion was a weak attempt to throw out over half of the passages. God graciously complied. OKAY. LET'S FOCUS ON WHAT THE NEW COVENANT HAS TO SAY ON THIS MATTER.

✺ ✺ ✺ ✺ ✺

---

4. Leviticus 19:19, 26–27.
5. Exodus 20:3, 13–15.

Pleased to have, at least temporarily, been granted the elimination of over half the passages, I turned to 1 Corinthians 6:9–10.

> Or do you not know that wrongdoers will not inherit the kingdom of God? Do not be deceived: Neither the sexually immoral nor idolaters nor adulterers nor men who have sex with men nor thieves nor the greedy nor drunkards nor slanderers nor swindlers will inherit the kingdom of God.

It specifically says men who have sex with men, and I'm a woman. Boom. So this one doesn't apply to me and Nora. Next.

> We know that the law is good if one uses it properly. We also know that the law is made not for the righteous but for lawbreakers and rebels, the ungodly and sinful, the unholy and irreligious, for those who kill their fathers or mothers, for murderers, for the sexually immoral, for those practicing homosexuality, for slave traders and liars and perjurers—and for whatever else is contrary to the sound doctrine that conforms to the gospel concerning the glory of the blessed God, which he entrusted to me. (1 Timothy 1:8–11)

This is just a list of people that the law was made for, it doesn't specifically condemn homosexuality. Plus, there are several descriptions in this list that apply to me. I am sinful, unholy, rebellious, and a liar. So even if this somehow does condemn homosexuality, then I'd be condemned already for at least four other things anyway.

Only one passage remained from the list of seven. I was so close to convincing myself I could be with Nora. My heart started to pound, and excitement shot through my veins. *Maybe, just maybe, I can prove to myself that the Bible doesn't actually say it's wrong to be with Nora.*

My final passage was Romans 1:24–27.

> Therefore God gave them over in the sinful desires of their hearts to sexual impurity for the degrading of their bodies with one another. They exchanged the truth about God for a lie, and worshiped and served created things rather than the Creator—who is forever praised. Amen. Because of this, God gave them over to shameful lusts. Even their women exchanged natural sexual relations for unnatural ones. In the same way the men also abandoned natural relations with women and were inflamed with lust for one another.

I felt like I had smashed face first into a brick wall. I read the intense language of this text over and over. *God gave them over . . . sinful desires of their hearts . . . degrading of their bodies . . . exchanging the truth for a lie . . . shameful lusts . . . unnatural sexual relations.* That last one hit the hardest. This Bible passage said it was unnatural to be with Nora.

In the very beginning of human existence God designed sexual intimacy to be between one man and one woman. Even our human anatomy points to the natural design of a man's body being joined with a woman's body. It is not the same for a woman with a woman, nor a man with a man.

I tried for thirty minutes to twist the words on that page to say something different, but I came up empty. No matter how creatively I attempted to change what it said, it simply says what it says. Whether I liked it or not was irrelevant to the powerful truth in those words: being in a romantic relationship with a woman is wrong.

After mulling and weeping over this heart-wrenching conclusion, I turned back to my laptop and wrote my response to God.

> Okay, Lord. You're right. Of course you're right. When I take your word by itself and read that passage, it seems undeniable to me. It seems so clear. Homosexuality is against your word and your design. I guess I can say I believe that with all my heart, but it just grieves my heart. I can't be with her, and I have to let go of the small sliver of hope that rose in my heart at the possibility of being together. But I know I can't let go of serving you, that has been the reason for my life since I was a little girl. Thank you for helping me find my answer. Truth be told, I think I knew it all along, I just really didn't want to believe it. I wanted to believe there was a way for me to have both, but now I know I can't. I won't let go of my dreams, my ministry, and my relationship with you all to be with her. If I can't have both you and her, then I choose you.

I paused for a moment to take it all in. In the big picture, I felt I ranked in the top ten most unfaithful followers of Jesus on the planet. Yet even I was unwilling to choose a relationship with Nora in the name of damaging my relationship with God. I couldn't do it. I took in deep, shaky breaths as tears continued to spill out of my eyes.

This was the hardest decision I had ever made. I had to choose Jesus. I knew serving him was the purpose of my life, and I couldn't exchange that even in the name of love. Even a love that felt so good and so right to me. God did not approve of us being together, and that was final. No matter what I thought or how I felt about it, that was that.

We don't get to just follow God when it's convenient, easy, or enjoyable. In fact, I believe it is in the inconvenient, difficult, and unenjoyable moments when our faith reveals its true colors.

Will I stand with God or against him? Will I live my life for Jesus or reject Jesus? There is no in-between. Being neutral is not an option because neutrality is an apathetic and lukewarm form of rejection.

Each person must make their choice. I made my first choice when I was eight years old. I made hundreds of additional choices to serve him and be for him throughout my life. And now I made a commitment yet again. I was committed to following him, even if it deeply hurt me.

I realized I still had a major unanswered question and started typing my dialogue with God again.

> So can I take this job? It seems like you flung this opportunity wide open for me. But I need to hear that you want me to be here. I don't want to just blaze forward without asking you about it. Is this job opportunity from you? Is this the right time for me to take on a position like this?

MY CHILD, TAKE A DEEP BREATH. I HAVE BEEN PLANNING THIS SINCE ETERNITY PAST. I AM ORCHESTRATING AND WORKING ALL THINGS FOR YOUR GOOD. EVEN THESE TERRIBLE DECISIONS AND MISTAKES I AM WORKING FOR YOUR GOOD. I KNEW HOW THIS WOULD PAN OUT, NONE OF IT SURPRISED ME.

AND I KNOW TO YOU THAT BEGS THE QUESTION: WHY DID YOU LET THIS ALL HAPPEN? WELL, YOU ALREADY KNOW THE ANSWER: I GAVE YOU FREE WILL. AND, YES, I DID SPEAK TO YOU BACK IN SEPTEMBER (TO TALK TO NORA AGAIN). I WAS GIVING YOU GRACE WHILE KNOWING IT WOULD BE ABUSED. DOES THAT SOUND LIKE ANYTHING ELSE I'VE DONE IN HISTORY?

"Yeah, the cross," I professed.

EXACTLY. THE CROSS. I EXTENDED THE MOST GRACE I HAVE EVER EXTENDED TO THE WORLD IN A SINGLE MOMENT, WHILE KNOWING THAT GRACE WOULD BE ABUSED BY MANY. BUT I DID IT ANYWAY. BECAUSE IT WAS WHAT WAS BEST. AND IN THE SAME WAY THIS WAS WHAT WAS BEST. I COULD HAVE KEPT YOU FROM TALKING AND SEEING EACH OTHER BUT THEN YOU WOULDN'T BE WHERE YOU ARE TODAY.

ALL OF THIS IS SHAPING AND MOLDING YOU FOR PLANS I HAVE IN STORE DOWN THE ROAD. BUT, FOR NOW, SIMPLY KNOW I DESIGNED YOU TO HAVE THIS POSITION, AT THIS TIME, WITH THESE YOUTH, AT THIS CHURCH. BUT AVERY IS RIGHT. YOU NEED TO BE HONEST WITH YOUR LEADERSHIP. TELL PASTOR DAVID I WANT YOU IN THIS POSITION, AND, WITH THAT BEING

SITTING AT A CROSSROAD

SAID, YOU CAN HAVE CONFIDENCE THAT EVEN IF IT ALL "BLOWS UP" THAT
IF I WANT YOU IN THIS JOB THEN YOU WILL HAVE THIS JOB. RIGHT?

"Yes, Lord. I trust you."

OKAY, THEN THERE IS YOUR ANSWER. TWO ANSWERS YOU ALREADY
KNEW, MY LOVE, BUT I WAS HAPPY TO TALK TO YOU ABOUT THEM. I KNOW
YOU LOVE NORA DEEPLY AND YOUR AFFECTION FOR HER IS GREATER THAN
ANYTHING YOU HAVE EVER EXPERIENCED. AND I KNOW MY ANSWER ISN'T
WHAT YOU WANTED TO HEAR, AND IT GRIEVES ME TO SEE HOW MUCH THIS
IS HURTING THE BOTH OF YOU. BUT THIS ISN'T MY WILL.

IT'S NOT MY WILL FOR ANYONE TO BE SICK, FOR ANYONE TO DIE, FOR
KIDS TO BE ORPHANED, OR FOR YOU AND NORA TO BE IN LOVE. THAT'S NOT
MY WILL. MY WILL IS PERFECTION. MY WILL IS TO SEE THINGS ON EARTH
AS THEY ARE IN HEAVEN. THAT IS WHAT I WANT. I DON'T WANT YOU TO
HAVE TO DEAL WITH ANY OF THIS SIN AND SUFFERING, BUT THAT IS THE
CONSEQUENCE OF ALLOWING THE ENEMY INTO THIS WORLD. WHICH WAS
THE ONLY WAY TO HAVE A REAL RELATIONSHIP WITH MY CHILDREN, JUST
LIKE YOU.

NOW REGARDING WHAT TO DO ABOUT YOUR FRIENDSHIP WITH NORA,
WE ARE JUST GOING TO WAIT ON THAT. SO LET'S JUST BREATHE AND REST A
LITTLE BIT TOGETHER AND THEN YOU CAN GO AND TALK TO PASTOR DAVID
JUST SIT WITH ME. I LOVE YOU SO MUCH, ADRIANA, MORE THAN YOU CAN
IMAGINE.

✳✳ ✳✳ ✳✳

I obeyed his words. I sat and rested with him. My heart felt completely
raw. Rawer than it had ever been in my life. This time of basking in his
presence was refreshing and healing to my heart. A supernatural calmness
fell over me.

Prior to this time of sitting with my heavenly Father I was beyond
anxious to talk to Pastor David—I was panicked. Now I felt an assurance
which could only be from heaven itself, and I resigned myself to the task
ahead knowing it was in my Father's hands. A Father who promised to take
care of me and work all things for my good. No matter the outcome I knew
my Father had it under control.

After delighting in the sweetness of God's presence, I got up to knock
on Pastor David's door. He stopped what he was doing and welcomed me
into his office with a cheery smile. His uplifting demeanor eased my fears,

at least a little bit. I sat down in a large blue-cushioned chair across from his desk. He bent forward with his hands folded in front of him, a posture of openness and active listening.

He maintained eye contact as I explained my situation. I kept it brief and vague. At the end I admitted, "This has been something I've acted on even recently. Recently, as in, like, within the past month." I wanted to be honest without having to be too specific.

After some questions and dialogue, he asserted, "As long as you are not presently acting on your desires or pursuing your sin, then I have no problem with it."

That was it. No elder meeting, no unnecessary details, no vote to determine if I was still fit for the job, and no shame. His assuring response provided relief beyond words.

He trusts me. Despite my story and my sin, he trusts me. At that moment I officially accepted the position as the new youth director at my home church. Not out loud, but in my heart. On paper I had accepted the job already the day prior, but now I knew I was truly committed.

I believed with all my heart this is where God wanted me to be. So even though it seemed a little crazy, I placed all my confidence in his good and perfect plan.

Chapter 14: Ending and Beginning

Even when you were running, even when you were hiding, [there's] never been a moment that you were not perfectly loved. When you barely believed it, when your eyes couldn't see it, every single moment you've always been perfectly loved.

—Rachael Lampa

My parents' motor home had been slowly sinking into the ground over the past seven years as it sat unmoved on their property. It stood untouched, tucked away in the woods, collecting dirt, and becoming a home for various woodland critters. Therefore, upon returning home from abroad, I immediately noticed it was missing.

I was informed a friend of our family, George, had a nephew in town who needed a place to stay for the summer. This nephew had cleaned it out, got it running again, and moved it into George's driveway—two miles down the road. A few days after starting my job as youth director, I ended up meeting this mystery nephew who was living in my parents' motor home. Well, more accurately, I re-met him.

When I introduced myself to him, he informed me he already knew me. During his childhood summers he sometimes stayed with his uncle George, and, apparently, he met me when we were little kids. I tried not to feel too awkward for not remembering him. It's easy to forget people when you are young, at least that's what I told myself to feel better.

His name is Brock. He stood at six feet tall with dark blonde hair in a stylish but close-trimmed cut. The gray T-shirt he wore showed off his biceps and shoulders. He had striking ocean eyes, a big smile, and a spunky, sarcastic personality. We hit it off right away.

A few days after meeting him, I ran into him after a church softball game. We played for different teams, but our games wrapped up around the same time. He informed me he and his family were all going to Dairy Queen for some ice cream, and he said I should go, too. I gladly accepted his invitation. I liked his family, I liked ice cream, and I was interested in getting to know him.

We got to the parking lot and started walking to our own vehicles when he said, "Hey, just wait a sec!"

He had ridden to the field with his aunt, and I watched in confusion as he went over to her car to set down his glove and water bottle.

"What are you doing?" his aunt asked him.

"Oh, I'm going to ride to DQ with Adriana!" he said cheerfully, and then jogged back toward me.

My eyebrows shot up. *You are, huh? Well, alrighty, then!* I tried not to read into the situation too much as this almost stranger, who I had not offered a ride to, climbed into my passenger seat.

We hung out at DQ for almost an hour. People trickled off until it was just me, Brock, and his two cousins. They later told me they only stayed to give Brock a ride back home. Eventually, one of them gave the ol' Minnesotan "Well, I spose . . ." to indicate it was time to leave. Brock's cousins walked toward their car while I strolled off toward my own, and, to everyone's surprise, Brock stayed by my side.

"Where are you going, dude?" his cousin called after him.

"Oh, Adriana can give me a ride home! It's basically on her way anyways!"

I can, huh? Well, alrighty, then! I smiled to myself at his forwardness in wanting to spend more time with me.

Our conversation flowed effortlessly from one topic to another during the ten-minute car ride. When I pulled up in front of his aunt and uncle's house, he didn't even unbuckle his seat belt. We just kept talking and talking.

"You know my aunt and uncle have a perfectly nice porch we could sit on to keep talking if you want?"

I was very much enjoying his company and agreed to his suggestion. We sat on a couch on their porch until sunset. The only reason we parted ways was lack of daylight and the mosquitos coming out. I smiled my whole drive home.

* * * * *

We ran into each other many times over the next couple weeks, and each time we parted ways Brock said, "Well, hopefully I'll run into you again soon!"

Finally, I told him it would be much easier to "run into me" if he just had my phone number. After that, he texted me multiple times every day. This resolved any remaining doubts in my mind that he wanted to be more than friends.

Our first date lasted nine hours because we didn't want to say goodbye. We had many more dates after that, had a "DTR" (defining the relationship) on the side of a road, and met each other's families. We talked for hours on end, we discovered each other's quirks, and he asked me to be his girlfriend while we wandered around a garden. I fell in love—this time with a man.

It happened fast. I always thought the phrase "when you know, you know" was annoying until I experienced it. For me, I knew that I knew through a prayer one day. November 20th, to be exact.

I was in the bathroom getting ready to start my day. While brushing my teeth, I was praying about my relationship with Brock. Suddenly the Lord brought to my mind my view of the purpose of marriage. I had developed this view during college and had repeated it many times to many people.

The only reason to get married is because you could better serve God together with that person than you can serve God separate from them.

I stopped brushing my teeth, spit out the toothpaste, and stared at my reflection in the mirror. Dumbfounded.

Whoa, wait a minute. I know, for certain, that I can serve God better with Brock by my side than I can serve him separately. That's it. This man fits my purpose for marriage.

I didn't know how to even begin processing this epiphany. I glanced down at my watch and realized I was running late for my morning staff meeting. I quickly finished getting ready and ran out the door.

My schedule that day was jam-packed. I didn't have time to think about my epiphany until I was driving home that night. I had the radio playing Christian music when a song came on that I had never heard. The lyrics were about the beauty of being fully known yet fully loved by God. As I listened to the words, I realized I could sing these same lyrics about Brock's love for me. Not because I worshiped his love, which would be idolatry, but because his love for me was already mirroring the love of Jesus.

One of the most exciting things about marriage is how it offers a new and better understanding of how Christ loves his bride—the church. The universal church, meaning all followers of him that have ever existed. Marriage is designed to reflect this love, and, even though we weren't married, Brock was already reflecting and displaying this depth of love for me.

God had provided two epiphanies in one day which led to the same conclusion: I wanted to marry Brock.

I had fallen in love before, clearly, but I had never said the words "I am in love with you." Actually, I had deliberately waited to only say those words to the person I would marry. The next day, I said those treasured words to Brock.

Nine months later, we got married.

※ ※ ※ ※ ※

Very early in our relationship, I shared about my relationship history, how recent it was, and how my heart was doing with it all. He was beyond understanding. In fact, God used Brock in my life to be able to write this book. Something I did not plan to do. He nonchalantly accepted my sexuality, and even enjoyed it, in ways I had never allowed for myself.

He provided the space for me to finally be comfortable with this piece of who I am. For the first time in my life, I fully accepted myself. I accepted both my relationship history and my present attractions. I realized I need not feel ashamed or embarrassed about these things.

Being attracted to women is simply one fact about me. I am also a snowboarder, I am half Costa Rican, I am a cool aunt, I am a softball coach, and I am a Taylor Swift fan. These don't define who I am, but they are part of who I am. Same with my sexuality.

I am bisexual. Some followers of Jesus are uncomfortable with that sentence because it says "I am." They fear this crosses a line when it comes to where I ground my identity. Admittedly, I don't need to use the words "I am," but it is a lot easier. I could say, "I have same-sex attraction," "I feel attracted to both genders," or "I struggle with same-sex attraction."

I could change my other "I am" statements too. I enjoy snowboarding, my ethnic background is half Costa Rica, I like to have fun with my nieces and nephews, I coach softball, or I like Taylor Swift's music. No one thinks twice about any of those "I am" statements because they aren't connected to sin. However, therein lies my issue, I do not believe being bisexual is a sin.

It can become sinful if those sexual attractions and desires are acted upon, but there is nothing inherently wrong about being bi. I am primarily attracted to women, and being attracted to a woman is no more wrong than being attracted to a man. It can become wrong, either in my mind or my actions, but the attractions are not wrong.

Feeling comfortable in my sexuality was tremendously liberating, and I found using labels to be helpful. After eight years of forbidding myself to say "I am bisexual," it packed a hell of a punch when I finally said it. It felt so good. However, I know this is not the case for everyone. This is a personal matter requiring a personal decision.

The simple truth is I see no issue in saying I am a bisexual woman. This feels right for me, but I don't need to convince anyone else that it should feel right for them. I also don't feel the need to convince anyone they should be comfortable with letting me say that about myself. It is entirely my own choice.

I will never proclaim a blanket statement for all queer Christians to use labels because they are liberating. They were liberating for me but may not be for others. For some, it is unwise and unhelpful. I fully support them in their decision to not use labels. It. Is. Personal.

My journey of growing increasingly more comfortable with my sexuality was a long one, but it started with a joke. Brock and I were sitting in my favorite room—the three-season porch. It is a porch off the second floor with windows on all three sides. We were chatting when, suddenly, he teased me in a way no one had before.

"Wait, did you just . . ." Smiling, I analyzed his face to try to read what was happening. I was genuinely searching to see if my theory was correct. "Did you just make a gay joke?"

"I sure did." He shrugged and smiled back at me. I stared at him, happily stunned speechless. I had never even considered he could be so accepting of my attraction towards women that he'd tease me about it. I loved it. I felt a sense of relief I didn't even know I needed. A relief which continued each time he helped me realize I didn't need to take my sexuality so seriously.

Prior to being comfortable enough to use the term bisexual I had opted for "I struggle with same-sex attraction." Oftentimes, I found myself whispering the same-sex attraction part of the sentence because I felt so terrible saying it out loud. Like it was an awful and gross thing that ought not to be said at a normal volume.

While being bisexual is not sinful within itself, I clearly had crossed the line from attraction to action several times with several women. However, I did not need to hang my head in shame over that anymore either. I had experienced significant freedom from the fear of what others thought of me, including what they thought of my mistakes and sins. I was, and still am, bisexual. I didn't need to hide that fact about myself anymore.

I had repented of my sin and was met by God's forgiveness. In all cases of genuine repentance, God, in his mercy, removes our sins as far as the east is from the west.[1] And since the east can never collide with the west this means our sins are entirely removed. The eternal consequence of my sin was paid for on the cross upon which Jesus died.

However, despite my eternal consequence being graciously removed, I still faced earthly consequences. Someone who repeatedly tells lies can be forgiven, but it is difficult to trust them. Someone who repeatedly steals can be forgiven, but they may be banned from certain stores or face jail time. My main earthly consequence is not being able to be friends with the amazing women I was once friends with until we chose to act upon our attractions.

The one which hurts me the most, obviously, is Nora. We cut off all communication a couple weeks after I started my job as youth director. But given my rapidly progressing relationship with Brock, I ended up reaching out to her a few times to keep her updated. I told her when we got engaged and even called to ask if she would be a bridesmaid in our wedding. As kindly as possible, she, understandably, said no to both being a bridesmaid and attending our wedding.

After sporadically staying in touch for a couple years, she ultimately decided it was in her best interest to go back to zero contact. To this day, I hope we can be friends again, but I recognize our broken friendship as a natural consequence of our choices. Plus, I do not believe a person can fall out of love. At least not completely. Thus, even if we were friends, it will always be complicated. Well, at least on this side of heaven.

* * * * * *

Brock and I have an incredible love story. It is more complicated than most because of my past relationships and the timeline of when we met, but there is so much beauty because of those complications. I loved falling

1. Psalm 103:12.

in love with him and he with me. I firmly believe God's hand was directly involved in the timing and development of our love story. Every step of it.

God was there when I tried to hold Brock's hand and he wouldn't let me in order to uphold our boundaries, when I told him I loved him for the first time, when we shared our first kiss, when he proposed to me in a hospital room, and on our wedding day. The day when the two of us became one.[2]

But even a love story as magical as ours is not the greatest love story. The greatest love story is not the one between Mary and George in *It's a Wonderful Life*, or Romeo and Juliet, or Jack and Rose in *Titanic*, or Mulan and Shang.

It is not the one between your grandparents, or parents, or your friend with a jaw-dropping extravagant proposal, or even your own—if you have one. The greatest love story ever written is the one between the God of all creation and the people he made in his own image.[3] His loving pursuit of humanity is written into every page of the Bible. His unconditional love is felt by his people every single minute of every single hour of every single day.

By far the strongest, most powerful, most meaningful, most life-changing love I have ever felt has been the love of God. That is the greatest love story in my life.

God was there with me in my darkest days, my proudest moments, my inner turmoil, my mistakes, my suffering, and in every relationship. He never left my side.

There are hundreds, maybe thousands, of songs about God's love for us. David Crowder Band compares his love to a hurricane and his grace to an ocean. Tauren Wells calls his love bulletproof and says we are fully known by God. God sees right through the mess inside of us, yet keeps pursuing and loving us.

Cory Asbury uses a controversial word and calls God's love reckless. He says it chases us down, that we can't earn it nor deserve it, and that it is overwhelming and never-ending. Stuart Townend says his deep love is vast beyond all measure. We are the wretches who he loved so much that he took on human flesh to die on a cross in order that we might be saved.

Jesus Culture sings that God's love is higher than the mountains, stronger than the grave, and constant through change. Hillsong Worship

2. Mark 10:8.

3. Genesis 1:27.

and Delirious? sing a song called "I Could Sing of Your Love Forever," and they repeat that phrase forty-three times.

Chris Tomlin sings we can't run from his presence or his open arms. And I know that full well because I tried to run, and I failed. His love was for me then, it is for me now, and it will always be for me. His love is for you, too.

Finally, Rachael Lampa sings the song lyrics quoted at the start of this chapter. She says, regardless of if we are running, hiding, unseeing, or un-believing that we have always been, and always will be, perfectly loved by God.

I have been perfectly loved by God every single moment of my life. For me, there will never be a greater love story than the Lord of all creation choosing to love me.

The love story between God and humanity is the greatest love story ever written and the greatest love story that will ever be written. And God—with that kind of deep, never-failing, bulletproof type of love—loves you. Yes, *you*.

Author's Note

M y chief aim in life is to bring glory to God and advance his kingdom. If you enjoyed my memoir and are interested in having me share a message with your church, leadership team, youth group, small group, camp, or any other group I would be honored. Below is my website. Please reach out if you are interested in connecting with me.

Find my contact information at:
adrianaforsman.carrd.com

Bibliography

Chapman, Gary D. *The Five Love Languages*. Chicago: Northfield, 1992.

Gilbert, Beth. "Do You Have a Codependent Personality?" Everyday Health, June 9, 2023. www.everydayhealth.com/emotional-health/do-you-have-a-codependent-personality.aspx.

Jones, Daniel. "The 36 Questions That Lead to Love." *New York Times*, Jan. 9, 2015. https://www.nytimes.com/2015/01/09/style/no-37-big-wedding-or-small.html.

Yancey, Philip. *What's So Amazing About Grace?* Grand Rapids: Zondervan, 1997.

www.ingramcontent.com/pod-product-compliance
Lightning Source LLC
Chambersburg PA
CBHW071444090426
42737CB00011B/1774